# Pryceless

## The Leon Pryce Story

AUTHORISED AUTOBIOGRAPHY

*with Aaron Bower*

GREAT-N-ORTHERN

Great Northern Books Limited
PO Box 1380, Bradford, BD5 5FB

www.greatnorthernbooks.co.uk

ISBN: 978-1-912101-66-5


Design and layout: David Burrill

Cover images: Stada Photo



CIP Data
A catalogue for this book is available from the British Library

# Pryceless

# Foreword

# by Daniel Anderson

Leon Pryce was a free agent at the end of 2005 when it came to my attention St Helens could have a chance of signing him from Bradford. Eamonn McManus, the chairman of the club, told me that he'd heard Leon was open to a change and asked me for my thoughts.

I knew I was a fan of his from afar and I'd watched him play in both club and international competitions and so I readily agreed to meet with Leon when I heard he might be available. I think we met at a TGI Fridays restaurant and my first impression of him definitely lived up to the perception I had of him from afar.

Although he was taller than I thought, he had a friendly - and very large! - smile and a genuine temperament about him. He instantly made me feel comfortable and he had won me over almost immediately. We signed him up as soon as we could.

On the field, I remember Leon cutting my own St Helens team - as well as other sides - to ribbons in the 2005 play-offs during his final games as a Bradford player on his run to winning both the Grand Final and the Harry Sunderland Trophy that year. Inside though, I was loving watching him, because I knew I would have the opportunity to get him in a Saints shirt the following year, in 2006.

We had some great players at Saints in the team in 2005, make no mistake about it. But we needed something different to go one step further in 2006 - so how about a 6'4" stand-off who could step off both feet, break tackles, score tries and run off the back of anyone who would pass him the ball? Yes, please. Come on down Leon Pryce!

We knew what we would get from Leon in a St Helens shirt from the TV performances we'd seen of him and the actual vision of him playing. But what you don't bargain for and what you don't see is the selfless team player who deferred to senior players in the team almost immediately. You don't see the funny Yorkshireman who would break the tedium of training with a joke, a smile or a comment.

You don't see a student of the game who knew other players. He knew their strengths and weaknesses and he also knew how to push the buttons of people to get them fired up when it truly mattered. Most importantly, you don't see that you're going to get a fella come into your club who can deliver game-changing pieces of individual brilliance that ultimately led to success in the biggest games on the very biggest stages. You just don't see all of that.

Of course, away from the rugby, Leon was definitely mischievous and part of the infamous 'Yorkshire Bus'. They all played the best practical joke I've ever seen on James Graham. I still talk about that to this day and tell people who I meet about it. It was a beauty! He was a cheeky impersonator, mostly at my expense! Although the other Antipodean guys in the dressing room also got it sometimes from him. Leon and Paul Wellens in particular used to take delight in impersonating my half-time sprays - even when they were on the receiving end of them! I know and remember there were some real funny moments.

But he was a guy who delivered the goods more often than not - especially when it mattered most. In the 2006 Grand Final against Hull FC - Leon's first season - we had identified a clear mismatch between Leon's brilliant athleticism and his opposing stand-off. We designed a play whereby Leon would receive the ball in the final 10 minutes of the first half, run at the left, outside shoulder of his opposing player, before throwing a dummy and blindly use his left hand to fend. It writes easy, believe me, but it's a ridiculously difficult skill to undertake when you put it into play for real. With the help of his teammates, Leon instinctively used all his talent and delivered the fend, before breaking the tackle and scoring the try to gather momentum for Saints in a tensely-contested Grand Final. As I say, he delivered the goods when it mattered most.

I also remember how many times he pulled us out of the fire. In the quarter-finals of the Challenge Cup against Hull KR at Craven Park, for example, he saved a try by holding up the fella when he had no right to - then scored the try which won us the game.

In 2008, Leon again broke the hearts of Hull FC fans when, late in the game, despite Hull securing a slender lead in the closing stages of the Challenge Cup final, it was his time to shine. In the space of 10 minutes, Leon had ghosted through the defensive line with that brilliant show and go of his before offloading to Francis Meli to score and help us regain the lead. He later sealed the final with a tackle-break and a solo try in front of the Saints fans.

The team at St Helens was a champion team that will measure up against any era in my opinion. And Leon Pryce achieved some wonderful individual and personal accolades, including winning the Lance Todd Trophy and being Players' Player of the Year at Saints. That's just to name but two - there were many more in a brilliant career.

What else is there to say? Leon Pryce loved to play rugby, and Leon Pryce loved his teammates. He did not, however, love to train! Although I will always remember that I loved coaching Leon Pryce every time we were together. You're a good fella and a bloody good rugby player.

All the best mate,

Gaffer.

# CHAPTER I

I came from a proper working-class family in Bradford, which I guess was the case for most people in the city at that time. Being raised by my mum, Janet, and my father, Denis, was great though, and we all lived in an area of Bradford called Bankfoot, which was a stone's throw from Odsal Stadium itself. It was your typical working-class upbringing. We lived in a three-bedroomed terrace house and I remember my parents were hard-working, honest people during my childhood.

Rugby was always going to be part of my life from a very early age, that much was obvious. My dad played for York during his earlier days, there's obviously my younger brother, Karl, who played as well as me, and my uncles Geoff and Steve also played professionally. Then you've got my cousin Waine Pryce, who has played at the top level for Castleford and had a fantastic professional career, and also played for England Schoolboys alongside me. So we're a very rugby-orientated family.

I was one of these kids at school who did a bit of everything sports-wise, because I just loved playing sport, it was my thing that I excelled at. I did athletics, football and all sorts, and my strength was PE. I couldn't sit in a classroom and be taught, but if you put me on a field it brought the best out of me as a person, in my opinion. Sport has always been my way of expressing myself. When I'm on a field running around, it's essentially my happy place.

I've played rugby since I was seven years of age. My first memories and experiences of the game were with a good mate of mine, Phil Weston. He's a lot older than me, but he used to come down and look after me, and he took me to my first rugby game, which was a Bradford Northern fixture. I was around seven years old, and ever since then the sport was sort of ingrained into me from that very first match. We'd go and watch away games together and he had a lot of influence over where I'm sat now, telling this story. It was him who got me into rugby and supporting Bradford Northern, as they were called back then. That was way back in the late-1980s when I first got into it, and my undisputed hero at that time was Ellery Hanley.

He's the person I first remember watching, and as a young kid growing up as a rugby league fan he was definitely someone I looked up to. Martin Offiah was someone I would class in the same bracket as Ellery. They made you want to lace your boots up and play rugby as well as watching it. They were inspirational.

But it was hard work supporting Bradford Northern back then. We'd go and watch them go to places like Wigan and St Helens away and you'd get absolutely walloped 50- or 60-nil. Compared to the Bradford that were around when I started playing, it was worlds apart.

People say their hometown club is the only one they'd ever want to play for, but if I'm being totally honest, that wasn't the case initially - it sounds daft now. Back when I started getting into rugby in the late 80s, Wigan were the top dogs. They had all the stars - like Offiah and Hanley - and when it came to me starting to pick up some interest as a teenager there were other clubs about that I considered as well as Bradford.

There was interest from Leeds, for example, when I got to about

14 years old. But it goes against the way I've been brought up to go and play for Leeds. I don't know what my family would have thought - I think my mum might have disowned me! Although I have a healthy rivalry with Leeds, I've got a lot of admiration for how they recruited back then. Look at the guys that they signed at a similar time to me: Danny McGuire, Chev Walker, Rob Burrow, Jamie Jones-Buchanan, Kevin Sinfield, the list goes on. It was a generation full of incredible rugby players who have done some brilliant things.

And even though some of my family might not have liked it, we did actually get way down the line with Leeds. I went for a few trials there and they clearly liked what they saw as they actually offered me a contract. Keighley also offered me a contract around that time. But it all changed when we got a phone call from Bradford - I can't remember exactly who it was - but someone rung my dad and he was saying, 'Don't sign for Leeds, you've got to come up to Odsal and speak to us.'

So me and my old man went up there with an open mind and we spoke to Brian Smith, who was brutally honest with me. 'I don't know what to say to you,' he said. 'I've never spoken to a 14-year-old about this kind of stuff.'

But crucially, he admitted he was interested and he urged me not to sign for anyone else no matter what. I remember the day well. We were cooped up in one of these little terrapin cabins at Odsal - I think it's where they have the club shop now - and his office was in the back of there. My old man took care of it all in terms of the contract and things like that. He's quite forceful and doesn't trust people too easily, so he took the lead. He was great with it.

By this time, I had been a fan of the club for a good few years and when push came to shove, it was the right decision and ultimately, it was an easy decision. At that time Bradford were just starting to get going. It was the days of 'Bullmania', Super League was just beginning and the club had just won it for the first time so they were on a bit of a high.

What also helped was that I knew Robbie Paul too. At that time he was our local hero in Bradford. He had become the big star of the team and he had quickly become my hero with what he did in the Challenge Cup, scoring the hat-trick at Wembley in 1996 against St Helens. I was in awe of him and he was all over the local papers. He was Bradford's poster boy. To get the chance to train with him and play with him was incredible, and he was a big part of why I signed too.

All those experiences with Phil were what got me supporting Bradford, but it was my old man who got me actually playing rugby. I was with Queensbury ARLFC, and then from there I went and played for Bradford Schools. We had a great team, but I remember we were always getting hammered against the likes of Wigan and Leeds. From Bradford Schools I quickly moved up to England Schoolboys, and I had the honour of becoming captain at 16. I played for the age group above mine at England, believe it or not, which meant I got to play alongside Kevin Sinfield at that level. He's a year older than me so I jumped up and was running around with him. We played France in England and then the following year at 16, I captained them on tour, which was incredible.

I remember being at training for England Schoolboys, and me being me, I was trying to impress a bit harder than everyone else. I'd been captain at Queensbury but I never got the chance to captain Bradford Schools and that really pissed me off! There were these kids from all over the country, you know them all, and I was trying to stamp a bit of authority on the team. I shouted at them all and tried to pull rank a bit, and the England coach turned round to me and said, 'I'm the fucking coach, not you! I'll tell them what to do!'

Eventually though, he gave me the captaincy and it's not until now, writing this book, that I can sit back and reflect on the fact that I captained my country, irrespective of the level. That's something I'm still proud of.

The support from my family was incredible and invaluable for me as a teenager. They went to every single game I played, went on tour with me and they've been to places like France to watch me play from a very young age. My dad was my coach at Queensbury and the support from home couldn't have been any better. They were very supportive of me all the way through my career. At home it was very disciplined and as a teenager you don't like that at the time, but I debuted for Bradford at 16 and you can't do that by messing around on street corners as a kid. I sacrificed a lot with friends but it got me where I am, and that's down to my parents.

I actually went to Bradford Bulls on work experience before it all began for real, though. I trained with them for a week and we had this one session I'll never forget. Odsal is famous for its terraces and back then, we used to have to run up and down them over and over again as part of our training - it was brutal!

When you're young you try and show you can handle the pace of it, but they made us go up and down the terraces for around 40 minutes. When we got to the top we had to get onto the tarmac and do some sprints, before getting in a circle and do loads of squats, around 100. As I walked away from that, I was that knackered my hearing went, I went temporarily blind and I was about to drop and faint. Thankfully I didn't but that was my first introduction to Super League training!

Back then though, all the older guys were really good with me. I'd been brought up to show respect to your elders and I think they saw that. I wanted to be around them all the time and be a first-team player like them, so people like Jimmy Lowes, Stuart Spruce, Bernard Dwyer and Brian McDermott were crucial for my introduction to life at Bradford and as a professional. If you were a cocky little shit back then, you wouldn't play, it's as simple as that. If you came in with fancy clothing and tried to look like a big-timer they'd kick you out - it was a proper club!

I'd been in and around the group for a year or so and I'd been playing Academy rugby when I was 15 and 16, and I was starting to think I'd get a chance sooner rather than later. That Academy team was still incredible and there were some great players, and that was the best time to be around.

You're living with your parents, you've got no mortgage, no kids, no responsibilities - you're just living the dream. I used to train, play a game and go out around the Queens Hall in Bradford with my mate Craig McDowell. When we didn't have a game we'd bugger off to Cumbria, because that's where he came from, and we'd go out on the Saturday nights and have a good night around town, before staying at Craig's mum and dad's house, who were really good to me - they looked after me. Those were the times I cherish the most, those brilliant teenage years.

But it was about to get even better. I was still at school in Thornton, combining that and playing Academy rugby, and I remember getting a phone call one day.

It was Matthew Elliott, the Bradford coach. 'Leon,' he said, 'I want you to come over to our training camp for a few days.' Brilliant, I'm thinking. Where is it? 'Lanzarote, it's a warm-weather camp.'

Result! I felt like I'd won the lottery. I was only 15 years old, being asked to go abroad with Bradford Bulls and to be honest, I don't think many of the kids actually believed me. A couple of days after that I was walking up to my ex-girlfriend's house, and there was a video store on the end of my road, so I called in to look at some videos to maybe take up there for her, like a bit of a romantic.

Then who walks in? Robbie Paul, and he starts talking to me like we're best mates. Lo and behold he ended up giving me a lift up to her house, and the next day I go back to school and started making out I was a superstar and telling everyone in my class that I'm good mates with Robbie when I actually wasn't. All he'd done was give me a lift! But that was a huge deal for me as a teenager. He is Mr Bradford Bulls. He's the number one guy since that club changed their name to the Bulls from the old Northern days, and he's one of the few men I'd trust with my life.

Robbie is one of the few people I look up to in my life with real admiration. I've got a relationship with him where if he tells me to jump, I would ask how high. I'd drop everything for him if he needed me to because he's been there for me throughout my career and my life.

He once presented a trophy to me when I was about 14 years of age and when someone treats you so well before you were nothing, you will do everything you can to help them when you are on the map, so to speak. He was my first rugby hero other than Ellery Hanley, and when you're a Bradford kid and someone is doing such good things for the city you live in, it's no surprise that I call him my idol.

I've made him godfather to my son and he's a guy that would give you your last pound. He's still my mentor now. He makes sure I represent myself in the right way. I turn up and do radio shows and keep my name out there and he makes sure if there's an opportunity for me, I take it. I see him as a bit of a father figure as well as a friend because he's guided me through my career and I can't stress how much respect I have for him.

I don't have that relationship with too many people. He took the brunt of everything for Bradford. If things were going well he would shoulder the responsibility for the team, and as captain of Bradford now while I'm sat writing this, I know I try to model myself on the way Robbie led Bradford Bulls on and off the field.

People love to stick the boot into Bradford, and all they talk about is the bad things that have happened like the Bradford Riots. Everything I read about my city was negative growing up, but suddenly this guy turned up, a fresh-faced Kiwi who has got swagger and doing nothing but good things for Bradford, and gradually, the city started to get good press. Bradford means everything to me, so when he's generating such good publicity for the city, I couldn't help but idolise him.

Anyway, at the age of 15 I'm off on my first ever trip away with the first team to Lanzarote and it was a dream come true. One minute I'm off to get my passport sorted and the next, I'm flying away with the Bradford Bulls players. It's the opportunity of a lifetime given how I was still only a teenager.

We weren't the only ones there either. The Great Britain athletics team were also there so we were mixing with the likes of Denise Lewis and Jamie Baulch. It was incredible and really weird at the same time!

Shaun Edwards was still around at that time, and one thing I really remember about that trip was how I used to have to run around, as one of the younger kids on the trip, and chase after the balls he was kicking around as part of his own training regime.

But what I really remember about that trip - on the field, at least - is breaking through a gap after a sidestep in a training game, and although I got tackled, I got up and got smashed to pieces by the guy I stepped - it was Paul Anderson, Baloo, who was massive and I was like a Twiglet at that time! As he went past me he said, 'Ey up, don't you ever step me like that again!' Needless to say, I didn't!

When you're younger you obviously are a bit more wet behind the ears to stuff that happens away on camps, and I was done a beauty by a couple of the more senior guys at one stage during the tour. I got a call to go up into one of the players' rooms at Lanzarote, and two of the guys were in there, Bernard Dwyer and Matt Calland, who are both really great blokes.

I obviously didn't have a clue what they wanted, and I didn't know they were about to properly wind me up! 'We want to see your cock - get it out,' they said, as you do! I was 15 years old and I was terrified, so I'm obviously saying no - and they said I either had to do that or down some whisky they had on a table.

That might have been a difficult decision for some people but it didn't take me long to work out what I needed to do. Without even giving it a single thought I went straight for the bottle of whisky and I finished it off, completely downed it, to try and impress them. Hopefully that would have made them forget about asking me to get my cock out I thought, but they still kept asking me afterwards!

I was shit-scared because I didn't know what was going on, so I burst open the back door and was going to jump out, but this jump was about 20 or 30 feet down to the floor - and this is all happening because I wanted to get away from them. As I was about to jump they screamed at me to stop, because they knew that with the drop I could have broken my leg, ankle or even died - it was that big. They were realising that they had put the frighteners on me. They tried to talk me down, but I still jumped and went onto this balancing beam and then onto the floor. Thankfully, I didn't get hurt. But it could have been much worse.

Being invited to go on that trip though, I had the feeling I wouldn't be too far away that year. That was 1998, but even then, to get the call was incredible. I never actually envisaged what it would be like getting the chance, but when injuries started to hit the club hard at the end of that season, Matty Elliott pulled me in and told me I'd be making my debut against Salford, at Odsal.

I woke up that morning - I say woke up, I didn't sleep one wink - and I was bricking it. My mum could see I was nervous, and she was hammering on at me about having something to eat. It was my first ever game as a professional, and what did I eat before I played? A big McDonald's meal! I was super nervous as anyone would be, and sat in the changing rooms, I was just wondering what the hell I was doing here, around all these incredible players.

Some kids get the chance to start from the bench and take it all in a little bite, but being a back, I was on the wing for my debut. Within seconds I remember thinking that it was a thousand times faster than anything I'd experienced before throughout all those age groups and everything - I just couldn't believe it. The one thing I remember more than anything about that game was getting a pass from Robbie and all I had to do was dive low and score a try on my debut. But again, me being me, I went to try and bump my opposite number off and I failed pretty spectacularly. But being the youngest player to play for Bradford was something I loved having next to my name.

Even when I was playing for them and in the Academy, I was still going up to watch the Bulls as a fan when I could. I remember that World Club Challenge game when they got hammered against Auckland Warriors, and I was sat there watching, cheering them on as a fan - not as a Bradford Bulls employee. The city of Bradford could sense something special was happening around that time though with 'Bullmania', and I'm privileged I joined them at the time I did.

Once I'd made my debut it felt like a proper box ticked off. 'Right, I'm a first-team player now, get in,' I remember telling myself. That year, we had a deal with Rover, the car manufacturers, and all the players were getting brand new Rover cars and I can remember thinking that I was going to break into that first team and Rover would be ringing me up and offering me a car.

I used to go into the marketing office and tell Debbie Charlton - God bless her, she's passed away now - that I wanted a Rover, and I must have sounded like a right cocky young git, but weirdly that's what I was focussed on. Unfortunately I never got one.

When 1999 came around I was playing in France for England Schoolboys, and I had to rush home on a plane to play full-back, and I got man of the match. I wasn't playing first-team around that time of course and given how Bradford were flying and everything was going great for them, I probably valued playing for the Bulls more than international rugby at that time, to be honest. It's always great to play for your country though and I'd never devalue it. I played in that England Academy game in France, playing stand-off alongside Paul Cooke in the halves and we walloped them.

I'm settling down after the game, then I get a call from someone at Bradford saying they want me to play first-team again. 'Shit, I'm in France,' I remember thinking. 'What the hell are we going to do?'

In a panic, we had to rush together some travel arrangements, so I flew back into Gatwick from France - that was the closest they could get me to home - before hopping on an overnight coach back to Bradford. So there I was, tired, having barely had any sleep, but ready to be thrown in against Wakefield. And, lo and behold, I go out and get the man of the match playing full-back.

From then on in I was in and out of the team for most of that year, and funnily enough it was Nick Zisti - a guy who the club had got in from Australia at the time - who was really struggling with injuries which gave me my chance. He ended up going to rugby union midway through that year and when he left, it just about opened the door properly for me to get in, make a spot my own and become a regular first-team player.

As I expected I was getting thrown around from pillar to post, playing full-back, centre and eventually settling on the wing - but like I cared at that time. I was living the childhood dream, the thing I'd dreamed about doing for years, playing for Bradford Bulls in front of thousands of people. Get in!

# CHAPTER II

Before my debut for Bradford and my so-called breakthrough year, I was on the YTS scheme at Bradford, a time I remember really well. We'd train through the week - this was combined with me being at school too - before going into other schools and teaching younger kids stuff. You'd do a personal training course at a school called Yorkshire Martyrs, with the club trying really hard to round us off as people as well as players. It was really rewarding, to be fair.

It was exciting because there was such a buzz around the Bulls and you all harboured the same dream when you were in the youth team. We had a great group of guys who came from all over: Castleford, Wakefield and everywhere across West Yorkshire who the Bulls had snapped up. At the time, they were the club people wanted to play for.

I expected to be there or thereabouts that year I broke through, but nowhere near as much as I ended up doing. I actually ended up winning the Super League Young Player of the Year award! The way the club made me feel and the people there, I knew that I'd be ready as soon as anyone went down with injury. Like I would go on and do later in my career, I played a lot of stand-off in junior rugby but I felt as if I'd studied the game enough to take any spot in the backline.

A lot gets mentioned about Bradford and how fantastic they were as a club in the days of 'Bullmania', and I've got to hammer home the fact that it is absolutely true, every single bit of it. The club generated such a feel-good buzz for the city and the way they handled the players - especially the younger ones - was something they can be very proud of.

I've spoken about the late Debbie Charlton already, and one time, I went up to her as this young, cocky teenager saying that I needed a car - not a Rover this time, just any car. Within a couple of days, Debbie would have three or four different dealerships with different price ranges, colours, everything. She made me feel like a rock star.

I had people coming up from London to watch me once, and I said to Debbie, 'Can you fix them up for me?' Within 24 hours she'd booked their travel, tickets and even a hotel for good measure.

Anything we needed as players, she delivered on. She became a manager for the players and it made you feel like all you had to do was concentrate on rugby. Who knows, maybe that was part of the success.

It makes the memories of the club so much better. It's not always about what money you're on or whether you're winning games each and every week. Sometimes it's about feeling wanted. Debbie was a big part of that, as were people like Steve Deakin, Matthew Elliott and Brian Smith - all the people that helped kick-start the club and turn it on its head when Super League began in the mid-1990s. The coaches and the players always get the headlines, but it's people like Debbie who make a club tick. She was the one who looked after us all. She was like a mother to us.

It was around the time I started playing for the first team that I took my driving test. I failed it first time, but I ended up driving around in Michael Withers' car without a licence most of the time. I actually got caught - but thankfully, not by the police. I was driving up the M606 when my dad's friend, big John, pulled up at the side of me. I quickly raced off once he realised it was me and later he said to my dad, 'I didn't know your Leon had passed his driving test.'

Obviously my dad was pretty mad when he found out and I thought I was going to get a hammering from him but he was okay. He just made sure I did the test again before I got caught by the police!

So without a car, I'd walk on to the end of my road and wait outside the chippy to be picked up by one of the ex-Bulls players, a guy called Tahi Reihana, before I could drive, with Robbie Paul in the car too. They were my travelling partners to get across Bradford as a teenager, and they were the best days, they really were. The laughs we had were incredible. And when I got to 17, things got even stranger.

Bradford had managed to land the services of Mick Withers just before all that, a guy who would obviously leave a fairly big legacy at the Bulls. He came over with no family and so off the cuff and without anyone really asking, I decided I'd go live with him over in Yeadon, on the other side of Bradford. He was lonely and needed someone to show him around Bradford, so I thought why not.

While we're talking about Mick and what he did for Bradford, there's a part of the 1999 season in particular that sticks out - the night where Mick became a bit of a Bulls legend with one kick of the ball.

We were playing Leeds and the buzz around the community was just incredible leading up to that, you could feel it. Those Bradford-Leeds games were always incredible but this time, things were even bigger in terms of the buzz. The club were making all sorts of noises about how they were going to smash attendance records for a Super League game and things like that and to be honest, I never doubted they'd fail. Over 24,000 packed into Odsal under the lights. It really doesn't get any better than that.

I remember being on the wing during the game and I was up against Leroy Rivett, who at that time had recently scored four tries in the Challenge Cup Final against London Broncos the year before. So me being a cocky little twat, I'm trying to make a name for myself.

'Right Rivett, I'm having you here tonight,' I kept telling myself. I went at him full steam to prove I was up there and able to hold my own against the top wingers, and at a later point in the game I remember having a scuffle with him and actually throwing him onto the tarmac around the edge of the pitch. Looking back at it now I was out of order, but at the time I was just young and hot-headed and looking to prove a point which is probably not the right way to go about it.

I was just caught up in the emotions as a Bradfordian playing Leeds. My rivalry with them has always been pretty fierce on the field and when I was younger I was really hot-headed, as that proves.

I remember that luckily in that game I got a try to get us back into the match when Robbie kicked through and I touched it down with Rivett right alongside me. I knew I'd scored it.

I just remember jumping up shouting 'I've got it, I've got it', and the players were mobbing me. Then Mick delivered with that late drop-goal, and after we hung on. Boy, did we celebrate that night. 24,000 there, a packed house, beating Leeds. What else can you say? Brilliant.

On the whole, that was a great year for the club and we played so well that we ended up in the Grand Final against St Helens. So here I am, a teenager, a Bradford lad, playing for the Bulls in the Grand Final. I can still remember to this day being told by Matthew Elliott I'd got the nod. It was a day I'll never forget, especially given how the game was on my 18th birthday.

I'd never played in a game as big as that, so it goes without saying that for most of the first half I was in Disneyland, or at least my head was. I wasn't even sure what was going on and it was totally crazy, but I remember Matty telling me at the break that it was my time to shine, and I certainly improved.

However, it's probably natural that the only thing I remember about that night is *that* moment with Mick Withers, as we had a controversial try disallowed at a crucial point of the game. It was a try, wasn't it, let's not pretend it wasn't! I'm running away thinking I've scored a huge try in a Grand Final and the feeling was incredible. All I know is I definitely scored it and if it was played in the modern era it would have been given. There was no evidence to suggest it wasn't a try in my eyes. Today, the advantage would have gone with the attacker. I don't want it to sound like sour grapes, but I think that was a crucial turning point in the match.

Of course we still had enough time to win the game from there but in my opinion, that was a game-breaking moment as far as I'm concerned. I'll never forget being stood on the field talking to some of the lads. 'I wish they'd hurry up and give this try, come on,' I'm screaming. 'I want to get on with this game because we're on top here,' and then I remember it flashing up - NO TRY. What? It produced this incredible sinking feeling I've only experienced a couple of times since throughout my whole career.

Believe it or not, we actually had a do for my 18th afterwards. Yeah great, just what I want to be doing after going through all that heartache and trudging off the field having lost my first Grand Final. The last thing I wanted to be doing was celebrating my birthday and I just couldn't speak to people all night. I was moping around and in truth, I just didn't want to be around anyone. I've played in a fair few finals since then and out of all the ones I've lost, not a single one hurts more than that one in 1999.

When you play in big games and you lose them, the disappointment is so crushing. When you're a teenager and you're so close it doesn't get any worse from a playing perspective. I knew we'd all have a chance to win it again so that wasn't the issue, it was just the way we lost it. We were the best team that year, but we lost it and it was so hard to deal with.

Even though we'd lost the Grand Final, I managed to win a fair few awards, and that was the icing on the cake for the year in general and the reward for all the hard work done at junior level. At that point in my life I felt like I'd worked so hard to get to that point, and my season didn't end there thankfully.

Shortly after the Grand Final, I remember getting a call from John Kear, who was the England coach at that time. He mentioned that Paul Sterling had got an injury and he wanted to meet me, and before I knew it I'm thrown in at the deep end and playing an international game for England against the French. Ironically one of the guys I was up against was Laurent Frayssinous, someone who would coach me much, much later in my career. We played them at The Boulevard and I managed to get on the scoresheet. It was another experience which rounded 1999 off nicely, but it could and perhaps should have been a lot better.

I was riding on a wave at that point and it was all amazing, but I was aware of how quickly it could come crashing down. In the year 2000, it certainly did that.

# CHAPTER III

Heading out of 1999 and into the new millennium, there was obviously loads of attention on me and I was that bowled over that I was still playing for Bradford I didn't even really care or think about going anywhere else. Why would I? I remember someone asking me and I pretty much asked them back why I'd want to leave my hometown club with brilliant coaches and players - it's a non-starter. Leaving was the last thing on my mind - we all felt like a family with the players, the coaching staff and, as I've already touched on, the people behind the scenes like Debbie Charlton.

Right from the start of the year I was being told that I was unlucky to miss out for Great Britain in 1999 and there was a World Cup coming up which I'd have a chance for, but I tried not to think about it. Being as cock-sure as I was in my own mind, I thought that if I delivered for Bradford again, that sort of stuff would take care of itself in terms of the 2000 World Cup.

There's always this talk about sacrifices young players have to make, like giving up on nights on the lash and going out all the time, but I had a different philosophy to it all. I'd been through school with three lads who I'm close friends with to this day: Gavin Buckley, Stuart Reardon and Jan Kwaitkowski. But when I got to the age of 17 or 18, I had to distance myself from them which admittedly was hard, but I loved rugby that much that it didn't feel like a sacrifice. I didn't start drinking until later into my 20s anyway, so I just got on with it.

Then around the time I was starting to break into the first team at Bradford my world changed when I met my future wife, Carly.

She's a bit older than me and we met in funny circumstances, as I was actually mates with her sister, Laura, who I went to school with since I was about 14. I remember Carly dropping Laura off at the bus stop one day and, me being the cocky little shit I was, I started winding Laura up saying I fancied her sister - you know what teenagers are like.

We used to go out to a place called JB's - it's not there anymore - back in the day in Bradford. Carly worked on the door there, so as I was old enough - or maybe a little bit before! - I got talking to her there, and we clicked straight away. I started going round to her house a bit more and I think her parents thought I was coming to try and see Laura, but it was their older daughter I actually liked. She's five years older than me so I always joke that she was a bit of a cradle-snatcher. The night we lost the Grand Final in 1999 she asked me to go up there to see her and the rest, as they say, is history. We were both young back then, dating and having fun and although she'd hate me to say it, the rugby always came first.

She's played a massive part in my life though, so much so that we're still together to this day, married with two amazing children, William and Lily. When I was 18, I got my own place in Wibsey, just up the road from where my mum and dad lived - we've lived there together ever since. It's not been easy. It's been tough because we had William when I was 21, so I was still really, really young. But Carly was awesome throughout all that and she helped me through being a father at such a young age and throughout all the rocky moments in my career and in my life. Since my nan passed away, Carly was the person I relied on for emotional support and stability. She became the number one person I trusted and without her support, I would have fallen apart. I've needed emotional support on so many occasions because rugby is a tough game mentally as well as physically, and she's been stood behind me holding me up and getting me through the tough times when I need her.

She does all the behind-the-scenes things: cooks for me, sorts my training gear out and allows me to focus on work and my job. It's been a partnership and a team effort to get this far and that's helped me as much as everything else. Throughout both court cases I've had to go through some turmoil and she was there, reassuring me and insisting she'd stand by me - and she never broke that promise.

But when injuries started to hit me and my game really hard in 2000 I just didn't see it coming. I felt on top of the world and it signalled the start of a really bad time in my life, to be brutally honest. The one thing I've always been good at is rugby. It was the only thing I could rely on and I knew I could draw plenty of confidence from playing the game. All of a sudden, I'm sat in a treatment room having to watch other people play. It had all been taken away from me, or at least that's what it felt like.

It wasn't just that, either. For the first time in my career I was getting a bit of criticism for some of my performances and I was being dropped now and again, and life started to get a bit real for me from thereon out. That's when you learn about yourself as a person, not when everything is brilliant and problem-free. I found 2000 quite hard on so many levels and I was still only a kid. I wasn't this 25-year-old guy who'd been playing for a few years. I was coming to terms with life at the top and after sailing through 1999, the following year was incredibly tough.

It carried over into life off the field, too. For the first time, I felt a bit vulnerable. I wouldn't go into pubs around the local area or clubs and I became so low on confidence it's horrible. People don't see it when you get flak from fans and fans come up to you in public and slag you off to your face. I'd consider myself a fun guy but I just couldn't deal with all that at 18 years of age. People would approach me and say stuff like, 'What's happened to you this year, you're shit'. How do you deal with that? The only way I knew how to do that is put a barrier up, so I wouldn't speak to people and became quite withdrawn, but then people start to think you're arrogant. The only way I could process criticism was by cutting myself off and I was in a very, very dark place throughout spells of that year. It was the biggest learning curve of my life because it made me realise that you need to be able to deal with the rough and the smooth.

I'd pick the newspapers up and would see that journalists were scoring me nine out of ten for games, and you start to believe the hype, you really do. Then on the flip side, you start to see criticism of yourself and you're getting marked four or five out of ten - and you question yourself. It's crazy really looking back, and I'd tell the younger version of me to stay away from the press and reading the papers, as you get sucked into it all. I learned a lot about myself. I had a lot of self-doubt and people think that life as a rugby player is all rosy, but when you get criticised after losing a game you carry that burden with you.

You're miserable when you get home, when you speak to people and you have that with you for a whole week until you play another game. For people like my parents, Carly and the people I directly dealt with, they got the brunt of it. It must have been a bloody nightmare to deal with.

I remember being dropped in the run-up to the Challenge Cup

Final in 2000 and as it turned out, I would end up starting that game at Murrayfield on the bench, which was surreal in itself. It was a moment which summed up the whole of 2000. It was tough to take and just wasn't great to go through. In all honesty though, I still feel like I was lucky to get on the bench that day. It turned out a rare highlight of the year with us winning the cup, albeit a fairly hollow one as I didn't feel like I contributed a great deal to the win. However, as you'd expect, we had a really good night when it came to the celebrations afterwards!

Somehow, despite having a real tough year off the field and an inconsistent one on it, I actually managed to get what people were tipping me for at the start: a spot in England's World Cup squad that year. Talk about ticking another box off. It was an incredible moment to be selected and one I'll never forget, but as was the case with most of that year, it would get a whole lot worse before it got better.

We got called up into the squad and we had a week's training in this five-star hotel, flying abroad to America on a private plane. We played the USA national in a friendly and beat them by nearly 100 points, we went to Disneyland and we lived the dream basically. We were going around like footballers. They actually shut the theme park down for us to spend the first couple of hours there on our own, which made us feel even more like celebrities!

When we got back it was quickly into business though, and we played Australia in the opening game, and I found myself up against Wendell Sailor of all people. I remember Adrian Morley smashing Bryan Fletcher into next week, and I nearly scored. Halfway through, I was thinking that these Aussies weren't actually that good. But after nearly scoring myself, we ended up losing the game 22-2. Typical, given what I was thinking earlier!

It was game two where all the drama happened for me though. We were playing Russia. We hammered them in the end when it came to the game, 76-4, and I scored a try, but near the end of the game I hurt my shoulder going into a tackle, and fell really awkwardly as I was coming out of it.

Straight away I knew something was up and they took me into the physio room and Chris Brooks told me it was dislocated - which I kind of guessed anyway given the pain. He gave me a shot of morphine and tried to pop it back in, but as he tried it, the pain was absolutely horrific. He had to give me another shot of morphine. He said it was enough to knock a horse out as it turned out. He eventually popped it back in and as I was getting a lift home from my parents and Carly, we went back to my parents' house and she had to look after me because I was like a zombie all night.

The worst was to follow, though. The day after - still pretty groggy from all the morphine - I had to go see a specialist and straight away he told me that I needed a reconstruction. Boom, just like that, your World Cup is over. That was about as low as it gets.

# CHAPTER IV

Having got over that shoulder reconstruction and battled my way back fit, 2001 was a strange year. I think it's easy to remember the success we had that year in winning the Grand Final, but it all started in really unfamiliar surroundings.

The club had decided to renovate and upgrade Odsal, which meant we were out for a couple of years, and we had to go down to Valley Parade, where Bradford City play. That was a bit weird to get our heads around to be honest, because suddenly we were moving to a different part of the city. But whatever, we just got on with it, and clearly it didn't impact on us that much.

You always want to play at Odsal, but in the grand scheme of things, it was a case of needs must for the Bulls at the time and with the good crowds we were getting back then, I suspected it would be great playing down there - and it really was. The crowd is right on top of you as the stadium is built that way, being a football ground. We had some belting atmospheres down there. I found it really exciting.

As the year rolled on, it began to get picked up on more and more that I was out of contract at the end of the year, and there was some interest picking up steam from the Rugby Football Union. But like I said earlier, at this point in my career my mind just was not on moving whatsoever. It wasn't an actual club who came in for me, it was the RFU themselves, offering to bring me over from league.

You've got to remember that the whole landscape of rugby union isn't like it was back then. Nowhere near as many people went as what they do now. There were fleeting conversations through agents but that was it. Why? I'll try and explain the best I can.

There were things in my head which I wanted to achieve in rugby league since when I was a little boy. I was 20 years old and I'd done pretty much nothing I wanted to do in my own mind. One of those was becoming a pivotal part of a team, and around that time, I was way off doing that. I'd never played half-back for a prolonged period of time, I'd never been and played at Wembley and I'd never won a Grand Final by this point. The checklist of things I had left to do was huge, so these rugby union links were always about, but for me at that time I just thought, 'What's the point?'

Ironically it was around this time - well, the following year in 2002 - when we went down to Twickenham and schooled those rugby union boys in the Middlesex Sevens. I played throughout the whole of the tournament and it was just great. What made it even better was that the night before, we'd actually been beaten by St Helens in Super League and I just remember being bundled on a bus down to London overnight, not having a clue what we were stepping into - but it was easy.

We absolutely smashed most of the teams we played in it, and we were just too skilful for them. I don't know how we'd been invited but I know Wigan had been down and won it before, and bearing in mind we were the Super League champions at this point, I have no idea why the powers that be thought it would be smart bringing a world-class rugby league team down to crash the party.

We were full-time professionals with systems that had been in place for years and they were only just turning pro, so they were on catch-up. It was a sign of the times that rugby league was actually in front of union at that point, and it's quite disappointing looking back because I think it'd be a different story these days. I reckon it would be a lot closer if something like that ever got put together again.

Shortly after all that, the deal was sorted with Bradford to stay for another few years, until the end of 2005. I had a few agents who were helping out but I didn't really like the way they were carrying on so I decided to take care of it all myself! It was just me and my dad who sorted it. No matter what the papers say about me at any time when I did or came close to moving, I never wanted to leave Bradford - even to go to St Helens initially. It killed me to leave Bradford when I left, because I could have stayed at Bradford for the rest of my career if I'd been given more of a sniff at half-back.

We weren't super-strict back then in terms of being professional and living the clean life - and boy did we take advantage of it at Bradford in the heyday. There were a whole bunch of us who'd go out and party near enough every weekend, and the fans were always out and about too. The Bulls used to have these functions at a place called Pennington's, in Bradford city centre, which has closed now, and there were hundreds of fans there most of the time. It was incredible, you were like rock stars. At that age, I loved that.

One week, we'd had a really short turnaround with our games - I think it was around Easter, but I can't totally remember. Nobby hauled us all in and insisted that we couldn't have a drink this weekend as we had a short turnaround. So what do you do when you get told not to have a drink?

You say that you won't but you end up being crafty and going to places where nobody knows you: your local pubs, or your houses and things like that - do not go out in town! Nobby was hammering it into us that we couldn't go on the juice, but something quite serious had happened with our winger Lesley Vainikolo's house - he'd been burgled, I think.

He'd obviously been on the lash after being burgled, and the morning after, Les was absolutely trollied when he turned up for training. When someone was absolutely hammered at training you used to hide them out of the way of the coaching staff and look after one another. But when someone like Les is pissed up in training like he was here, how do you hide him? He's massive! We could smell beer on him the next morning so we packed him off to the back of the room to try and keep him out of the way.

So here we are, hauled into training the next morning after a game to do our video review, and Les is one of the worst people in the world at hiding it when he's had a drink because for some reason, he stays pissed the morning after and it's so, so obvious. We went into this video meeting to prepare for our game and look back at what we'd done the night before against Leeds, so we're trying to keep him quiet at the back of the room because Nobby was going ballistic. I think we'd actually lost the game against Leeds, if I remember correctly.

He's going barmy about this game and everything we were doing wrong, and at the end of this lengthy video review he looks around the room when he asks if anyone wants to speak - and Les puts his hand up. Straight away we all look at each other and fear the worst because we know what he's like. Turns out we were right to be worried.

Nobby is really giving it to us, and he asks, 'Has anyone got anything they'd like to say in response?'

That really wasn't what he wanted to be asking with Big Les in the room still tanked up, and he puts his hand up and says something which I will never forget:

'Hey coach,' he goes, 'I had a drink last night and I don't give a fuuuuuuuck!'

The whole room just went into meltdown and we were crying with laughter, although we didn't want to laugh too loud because Nobby was raging by this point and we didn't want to upset him even more. It was like we were going against the coach but Les was a larger than life character and Nobby knew how to get the best out of him because he almost fathered him after bringing him to England. He really did look after him and a few of the other overseas boys.

Anyway, we all stood up to walk out and go out onto the field and Nobby called Les back to haul him into his office. Les' face dropped because he knew he was going to cop it and straight away he was trying to grab a few guys to go and face the music with him. He turned to big Joe Vagana, I think, and pleaded with Joe to get him in with him, but Joe wasn't having any of it - none of us were. God knows what Nobby said to him but that's one of my favourite moments regarding Les - although there are a fair few to choose from.

I feel compelled to get him in this book because his partnership with Shontayne Hape was sensational. Robbie did everything for the club and put Bradford Bulls on the map with stuff like the hat-trick at Wembley and things like that. He's so inspirational for me as a Bradfordian who loves rugby league, but just behind him, Lesley Vainikolo is right there. He was unbelievable.

It was the way he acted and how nice he was which was the best thing about him. I could bring him out with all my friends and they absolutely loved him. He'd fit into any crowd and he'd just be the guy that had everyone in stitches all night long. He was harmless when push came to shove and he was the epitome of how good the times were at Bradford.

He was a serious freak too. I remember when we'd just signed him, we went off on a training camp to Portugal and we had a bit of a practice game to ease us in. We were both playing on the left wing so we were on opposite sides, but he made a break. I was seriously quick at this point - I could have matched Usain Bolt, or maybe not! So straight away, not really knowing too much about him, I thought, 'He's a bit of a big lump, I'll catch this guy no problem.'

I don't think I've ever been more wrong about anything in my entire life. I was going full pelt and I put the afterburners on and I remember just thinking that I was getting nowhere near him and he was still accelerating away from me.

'What the hell is happening? I can't touch him,' is racing through my mind, as Les gets further and further away from me. I've never seen a human that size move like that - you talk about him being a freak, well this was the moment I realised it.

I thought something was up with me initially as he blistered past me - and he's massive - and I didn't have a clue then what sort of animal we had on our hands. When he was in shape he was the ultimate freak of nature. He's not far off being one of the best players the Bulls has ever had when push comes to shove.

Guys like Lesley, the culture we had and the togetherness was what got us a long way in the early years of the 2000s when we were dominating the world of rugby league, not just Super League. Some of the guys used to jokingly dub me the 'Prince of Bradford'. I'm not really sure why, but Robbie was the King of Bradford, wasn't he, so I could never be the King! I was close with Robbie, and with my nickname being the 'Fresh Prince' - they used to play the music before reading my name out at games - people used to call me that and I think it's still stuck with a few of the boys to this very day.

The team was full of characters back then though, not just one or two. We used to go out through the week sometimes as a big group, and we'd go over to Ossett, where Henry Paul lived. We'd go out drinking midweek sometimes - although I wasn't drinking back then, honest, I just wasn't that into it at that time - and there would be some big sessions if we were playing Sunday, because Tuesday night was a long way until the game.

Anyway, this one time we all went out and I left them in Ossett, and the next day, something had clearly happened because HP turns up at training the following morning with this ridiculous pair of sunglasses on. Bearing in mind it was pretty gloomy and we were in Bradford - where it's never sunny - I immediately knew something was up, and he actually tried to do a full training session in these sunglasses without admitting to people what was happening.

We eventually managed to convince him to take them off at the end and he had this massive black eye. Turns out he'd been hit by someone in a boozer in Ossett! Nobby saw it and was obviously livid. Anyone else would have been dropped, but not our Henry. He was on another level to be fair, we couldn't have afforded to drop him back then because he was incredible for us.

In 2001 we had managed to battle our way back to Old Trafford for another Grand Final, but this one was different. In 1999 we were heartbroken and beaten in the worst way possible, but this time, we absolutely annihilated Wigan, beating them 37-6. Given everything that had happened two years ago I was expecting to be more nervous but actually, I was way more relaxed. I knew what to expect of the whole week and the build-up to the game and it definitely helped.

The final itself was bittersweet for me. I'd been having a great game from what I remember and I was really in the thick of it despite being on the wing, but in a pretty innocuous challenge just before half-time my ankle got twisted underneath me, and I had to come off injured. In essence though, we'd won the game by half-time because you don't generally have big margins in a Grand Final - and we were 26-0 up and cruising. It was incredible. Mick Withers got himself a hat-trick and we were unstoppable. Winning it when that full-time hooter went was just like a massive weight lifted off my shoulders, because it was the realisation of one of my lifelong dreams. We didn't just win it, we'd won it in style and after losing a couple of years earlier, it was the best feeling.

Luckily I went on to win a few more of them and get some more Grand Final rings, and I did different stuff with them. I gave one to my dad, and I actually gave one back to the Bulls when they were in big financial trouble. In essence all it did was just go a way towards writing off someone else's debt, which was a shame. It went for £5,000 too. The other two are at home. They're mine and they're not going anywhere.

That year ended with another big box ticked off too: getting the call to play for Great Britain. It's funny because in some sports all you dream of doing is playing for England - like football and cricket and stuff like that - but in rugby league, for me at least growing up, it was all about playing for Great Britain. Growing up, watching the likes of Ellery Hanley and Martin Offiah was inspirational. It's where my childhood memories were formed. To get the call at the age of just 20 was incredible - then you factor in who we were playing that year.

Games against Australia, for me at least, is where the whole intensity and hype of the sport jumps up a notch. It's funny because, like I've mentioned before, I wasn't filled with a huge amount of pride back then because it felt like a natural progression through the ranks, but looking back, wow. Nowadays I can sit back and think I reached the pinnacle in playing for Great Britain.

The main thing I remember about the first game at Huddersfield was the performance of Paul Sculthorpe. He got the man of the match, scored two tries and, bearing in mind we were playing the almighty Australians, I remember thinking that Scully was on another level to every single person out on that field. He absolutely destroyed them and it was fantastic to play alongside a legend when he produced such incredible form. It's very rare that with us all being full-time and playing the same game, someone is just so much better than the rest. That was Scully for you, though - he was a phenomenon.

The 2002 Grand Final was another moment in those early years at Bradford that sticks out in my mind because it featured another big game-breaking moment, just like in 1999 - and I hate mentioning it to this day: the dreaded voluntary tackle. It was a crazy game and Sean Long kicked St Helens ahead in the dying minutes with a drop-goal, I think that made it 19-18 in their favour. So frantically, we got going again and we were right on their line when Chris Joynt just dropped to the floor without any prompting. We all looked around and wondered what the hell was going on. 'Voluntary tackle, surely,' we're all shouting at the referee. Well it was, I don't need to leave that one open to debate!

So we all expect we'll get a penalty because he's hurled himself to the ground, but the referee just decides to let play go on and amazingly, they end up closing it out and winning the game. It hurt, it really did. We thought we'd have a nailed-on chance from in front of the posts to win the biggest game of the year - and bearing in mind it would have been Paul Deacon taking the shot at goal, there's not much chance he was missing it, let me tell you.

There's a massive moment right there. No one loss hurts me more than the 1999 Grand Final with the pass involving Mick Withers that was chalked off and it haunts me still to this day, but boy, 2002 still stings a little bit looking back when I mention it. 1999 kills me, however. Luckily, we'd get at least a couple more before my time at the Bulls came to an end a few years later.

# CHAPTER V

I've made plenty of references to some of the most important people in my life throughout this book, but I only felt it right to dedicate a whole chapter in itself to those who really matter most: my family.

I had a massive amount of support from my family growing up and I think that was the reason for me doing as well as I did when I was so young. Some kids don't get any support and they're left to do it on their own. I'm not sure I'd have got anywhere without my parents, so I would just like to take this opportunity to thank them for that. They've been incredible.

I'll start with my dad. He was more than a father to be honest, he was a mentor and a coach and essentially an inspiration for me. He got me on the right track with my career from a young age, took me to every game and he and my mum would watch me home and away wherever I played.

He was a rugby man too. He played for York and then for Great Britain BARLA, so it was pretty obvious rugby would be the sport I might end up being decent at. Plus, my uncle Geoff had a strong career in the sport too, and another one of my relatives, Steve, was the same. It's in the blood is rugby league among us Pryces.

Obviously I'm not the only Pryce brother, there's my younger brother, Karl. With us both being from Bradford and obviously being brothers, it was quite a point of pride for me to get to play with Karl when I did at Bradford.

As brothers, it might surprise some people, but we didn't speak to each other every day or spend much time together. We're very much the opposite and we're two different people. Karl is a very laid-back, chilled out kind of a guy who takes anything in his stride. If he was any more laid-back he'd probably fall on the floor and die!

I'm quite highly strung, moody and I'm quite aggressive with a lot of aspects of my life. Karl has always been a bit of a mummy's boy. He won't like me saying that! There's been a personality difference from an early age, so we were never like Henry and Robbie where we saw each other every day. I'm a little bit more like the big brother, where I'll look out for him and I want the best for him, so to see him follow the path I've been on and make his way into the first team at Bradford - that is something I still look back on with a lot of pride.

In rugby, if you recall these memories sitting here over a decade on, it's not until now where you're very proud of it. I guess at the time it wasn't something I thought about because I just expected it. I knew he was a bloody good player, and I knew he was bigger and stronger than people around him who were his age and I always pretty much thought he'd make it at the top level. Now, we can look back together and realise that we played in the same team as our brother and think that was a pretty cool thing to have done. I'm certainly proud of it.

It might have been tough for him coming into the team after me - not because I was amazing, more because he had the surname and I'd broken into the first team at the Bulls. But the way I was as a brother, I would never put my arm around him.

I'm very hard on people like my children and my kid brother because I expect a lot from them. I don't mollycoddle my children. I just know what people are capable of and what they can do and I certainly knew what Karl could do - although I understand it was probably hard being expected to simply follow in my footsteps.

He had a different kind of pressure to me because I made a name for myself from scratch and it's something I'll have to look out for with my son, William, if he ever starts playing rugby at a decent level. But I think it's nice to make your own name in the game. Henry Paul was an amazing player, but Robbie made his own name at Bradford - and I think Karl definitely did that too, which was good for him.

Outside of my mum and dad, the person I was closest to was my nan and I couldn't have written this book without mentioning her because she was a special person. She spoiled me rotten and she was the one grandparent I had the closest relationship with growing up.

We were really close and when things weren't good at home or things would get a bit stressful with school, friends or rugby, I would go and see my nan and she would make me feel so much better. I'd see her once a week and it continued that way until she passed away a few years ago. I owe a lot to her for the way she treated me alongside my parents and I owe her and my grandad a massive amount of debt for the role they had in my upbringing.

If it wasn't for them, I wouldn't be sat here writing this book right now, without a shadow of a doubt. It's sad that she won't be able to read this book, but her name and the role she played in my life will forever be documented in this book in terms of how much she meant to me - and I'm glad everyone can see that.

My upbringing itself was pretty ordinary, I went to two working-class schools in Marshfields First and Wibsey Middle in my local area in Bradford, before meeting my best mates who I'm still mates with now in Gavin Buckley, Stuart Reardon and Jan Kwaitkowski. We've formed a friendship that's lasted such a long time I would class them as brothers rather than friends.

We weren't exactly naughty or badly behaved at school as a group, but we were certainly mischievous. I wasn't allowed to be bad because my dad would come down on me like a ton of bricks if he found out I was mucking around, believe me! He was a big man who I was a little bit frightened of. I wasn't in a position to be naughty because I was fearful of my dad. But that was good. He made me understand quickly what it was like to do things the right way in life.

Obviously my friendship with Stu is quite well-known given how we both played together in the public limelight, but they're all amazing blokes and I can't speak highly enough of them. We learned how to stick together from an early age. You can't buy that. I think it's quite special to still have the best friends you had as kids 20 years on.

Unfortunately, they all went to a different school when we got to a certain age, Buttershaw. But it didn't have the best reputation. It was the school that they used to film Rita, Sue and Bob Too in Bradford though, weirdly! My parents wanted to send me to another school, Thornton. I remember being absolutely gutted, but being away from my best mates toughened me up a little bit as well. That was the best part of my childhood growing up, learning so much at a young age.

Around the time I signed for the Bulls - I think I was about 15 - I needed to get my own bank account for the money that was going to be transferred to me as payment for being on the Bulls' books. I never had one up until that point, so I went and sorted it all out and when I came home from school one day, I noticed a letter on the floor and for some reason, it had *'Leon's Birth Certificate'* written on it.

So I opened it up thinking it was to do with me setting up this bank account and when I had a close look through it, it said my mother was Janet Whitaker, but my father was someone else. At the time I didn't have a clue what was going on, so I waited for my mum to come home and I showed her and said I started wanting some answers. She read through it and admitted she had some explaining to do.

She pretty much revealed that the man who I thought was my biological father - Denis, the man who had brought me up - wasn't my dad in actual fact, and some guy who I'd never even heard of, let alone met, was my biological father.

To be told that at 15 years of age, your life gets turned upside down. Even though it can affect some people in different ways, it was quite important for me to know. I was hormonal as hell as a 15-year-old anyway, and it had a profound impact on me because it made me more withdrawn and made me a little bit more quiet, on the whole.

It had a big effect on me. My brother didn't know and I made them tell Karl so that there was nothing being hidden and nothing was being kept in the dark from my kid brother. Why have more secrets after this was being kept from me for 15 years? It must have been a real burden on all my family to be honest, so I just wanted it out there. He was a little bit upset when he found out of course, but I just didn't want him to find out via anyone else or any other way like I had. I said they had to tell him or I would tell him - and they chose to.

It's not something I'm ashamed of - and I don't really see why any of my family should be ashamed of it to be honest, especially my mum. I can understand why it was so hard for them to tell me because all I'd done is grow up with my dad - and I won't call him anything else other than that - thinking he was my biological father. I suspect that no kid ever actually wonders whether the people who have brought them up are actually their biological parents, so I never gave it any thought growing up.

What they all failed to realise though is that it just gave me so much more respect for my dad. I decided to think about it like this: he took me and my mum on when I was about 18 months old, so for a man to come into her life at a time of need when she was on her own with a young toddler - well, what a brilliant bloke. There aren't many guys like that around, and he is a great man for what he did. He didn't have to take me on and bring me up as his own, did he? But he did. And he's my dad no matter what a piece of crappy paper says.

I wouldn't be playing rugby without his influence, so I wouldn't be sat here now today telling this story. It didn't make me think any worse of him. Of course I was upset that he didn't tell me, but I could understand why he didn't say it until it had to come out the way it did.

It still upsets me how I found out, without them sitting me down until I asked them some questions. But it gave me infinitely more respect for the thing he did when I learned all about it. That's something that happened in my life that impacted on me really heavily but you've got to learn to move on. I've never met this other bloke and to be honest, I don't want to. My dad is my dad and I'll never refer to him as anything else. I want him to know just how much he means to me and how he'll always be my dad. It didn't change my relationship with him or anything like that, but it's a pretty important moment in my life looking back.

Mine and Karl's relationship has always been pretty standard, if not completely close. There's five years between me and him, but I've always tried to look after him as a big brother. I love him to bits, but we've not had the relationship some siblings have. The age difference is a big part of that and we're different characters. He's so laid-back and chilled out and I'm quite intense. We've never not been friends, but we're not like the brothers who spend every single day together.

I had lots of mentors in my life, but that started from an early age. I had quite a strict upbringing with my mum and dad, who were very disciplined people and they certainly brought me and Karl up properly. I was an older figure for Karl to be a bit of a mentor for him. We're a lot closer now because life was mostly about rugby back then and about how Karl was following in my footsteps and stuff like that. I always tried to make him sure that he could be his own person and not have to emulate anyone or copy anyone just because of his surname.

As we've grown up and had kids - and I've chilled out a bit - we're closer than ever.

I realised throughout my career that there's a lot of fickle people out there. I always say that there are two types of people who come through the terraces: fans and supporters. You want the supporters because they're the people who will support you no matter what - both yourself and the team. You could be playing crap, the team could be losing and all things like that, but supporters are always there, win, lose or draw.

They're the guys you need as a player, but there's the fans - who I'd class as the people that will love you when life is brilliant but when things are a bit rough, they're the first to jump down your throat and say you should be sold, or you should be dropped, and things like that.

What they don't realise is that you could have all sorts of things going on. You might be playing injured, you might be playing with injections or even worse, you could have some real problems going on in your life off the field and people sometimes can forget that rugby players are human beings as well.

There's a lot of circumstances why you might not be playing well, but fans don't want to know that, they want to simply see you play well - and fair play to them, because they pay their money and they deserve to see the best of you, I suppose. But after a game you go home and you see your children, your parents, your close family and your wife, and it makes everything perfect again because they love you no matter what.

It must be horrible going through your career without a family as a rugby league player, because they are your rock, and they're the people who remind you that everything is good in the world, even if you've had a crap game of rugby here and there. I tend to hold those people very close to me and after getting hurt a bit when I was younger by people - people treat you on how you were performing on the field rather than the person you actually were - it toughened me up. Those people can turn on you at the drop of a hat, so I knew I'd be best sticking to my close circle and not really bothering with anyone else. Their opinion was all that mattered and if I had a bad game, they wouldn't turn their back on me.

You get a lot of attention as a rugby player and at a young age you really tend to love that because it's quite flattering. But suddenly, you're in the public eye and everyone wants a piece of you. It was amazing, but you learn when you mature to take things with a pinch of salt and be a bit more humble about things. It took me a while to learn how to deal with those situations and not try and be mates with everyone. If I could give any advice to some younger players it would be to just be careful being out and about - and don't take your family and close friends for granted. I don't know where I'd have been without mine and they were vital as my career began to really take off.

They were also there when I needed them most when things went wrong.

# CHAPTER VI

*In September 2002, I was involved in an incident in a Bradford nightclub which resulted in me later being charged with unlawful wounding. A year-long high-profile court case, in which I eventually pleaded guilty to the charge levied at me, saw me sentenced to 120 hours of community service.*

*Out of respect for both the defendant and his family, I made the conscious decision that the incident itself is something I didn't think was right to discuss. However, the aftermath of it, the battle in the courts and how it impacted on my life during and after the case's conclusion is something I am keen to share.*

We all do things in life that we regret but it's those things that make you the person you are today. I don't think you truly learn unless you make mistakes. I'm not saying you should make mistakes, but I've paid for mine and it's made me a better person in the long run. It's cost me a lot of money and caused me a lot of stress along the way and I wouldn't recommend it to anyone. I've got two kids and if they look on the Internet and see these things that have happened which I'm not proud of it's really not good.

But Bradford were really good with me throughout it all. They said that if the worst happened and I went to jail for it all, they were going to keep me on an almost scaled-down contract to help my family pay the bills while I was inside. There were media reports saying that the Bulls were going to tear up my contract. I suppose they could have done that legally, but when Brian Noble was there to help me deal with it all from the rugby side of things, I couldn't have asked for a better coach and a better person to stand by me in that role. It was one of the reasons why I didn't want to leave. They stuck by me throughout and the support they gave me was huge, because I'd done something which brought the club and its name into disrepute. I'm really grateful the Bulls lived up to their reputation as a family club and took care of me.

I'd effectively brought the club's name and its reputation into disrepute, hadn't I? I was in an ugly off-field incident and as a player who billed himself as a proud Bradfordian and someone who was proud to play for Bradford Bulls, this didn't make the club look great in my eyes. But they gave me a world of support and they were incredible, if truth be told. They really stuck by me. They were fantastic and they didn't have to do it.

I was wrong with what I did, there is simply no getting away from that and I wouldn't want this book to suggest anything otherwise. It's vital people understand that. But as a club, Bradford really looked after me and I've got to say that they supported me incredibly well throughout it all until the case drew to a close, which was important for a young lad who was just 21 years of age at the time it all happened.

From start to finish, the whole thing lasted a full year, which was obviously a long and difficult period for everyone involved. Thankfully, rugby was my escape and it was my release - it was just the rest of my life which was a problem at that time obviously. On the rugby field I was getting booed a lot more but I could deal with that. The problem was the abuse my family was getting - and that was tough because they couldn't control that.

When it happened a lot of people thought I was lucky to escape jail and maybe that's the case, because people have been to prison for things like this, but right up until the day of the sentencing I was expecting and anticipating that to happen. I even took my washbag with me to court planning to not come out of that courtroom without going to prison in the back of a police van.

My parents couldn't speak about it, and not many people could in my family. They were all too upset and we're not the best of talkers as a family anyway. Me personally, my head was in the clouds and I was so out of it, almost spaced out with it all. I lost all my confidence in myself and I just shut myself off from the world, and I didn't talk to anyone for a full year about anything close to my heart. When you're in your local area and you're getting talked about and people make their assumptions you get pre-judged, and that's where it's difficult for your family especially; and where I really felt it. You've go to deal with that on a day-to-day basis, and so does your wife and your parents. Jeez, that's just horrible and something I feel sad I put them through right to this very day.

My barrister, who was brilliant with me throughout, pulled me aside one day up in Teeside Crown Court where the trial was - because I couldn't have it in Bradford, where I was known - and said that if I pleaded not guilty, went ahead with the trial and got found guilty I'd get five years in prison.

He said I could plead guilty to a lesser section and if things went well, I'd get six months. My two choices were to fight the case or plead guilty and get a lesser sentence and there were a lot of tears in that room when that discussion took place, because it all hit us at once and we had to decide what we were going to do there and then.

We weren't sure initially and Carly had just had William, so he was only one. In the end though there was only one thing to do and we went with the guilty plea because it happened. I held my hands up to the fact I did wrong and I still know that to this day. As it turned out, I got sentenced with 120 hours' community service and £700 worth of costs.

How it impacted on me for the rest of my life is probably the big thing I took from it all. After that happened and I got whatever punishment I got from the courts, I was a different person. I was a vibrant, outgoing person but after everything that happened it spiralled me into a bit of depression.

People were judging me before they knew me, thinking I was a bad guy and inside my own head I started to believe that. I started to be convinced I was a bad person. People think you've got off lightly because you haven't gone to jail, but I carried what I did that night with me for a good 10 or 11 years before I could really begin to let it go. You hold it against yourself and it made me a really defensive and guarded person and it's completely changed my life forever - and I probably deserve that for what I did.

It made me worried and apprehensive about going out in my local pub. I'd get really nervous going in a pub in Wibsey, where I lived, called the Ancient Foresters, which sounds ridiculous looking back. But because I come across as loud and very opinionated, people think that you're like that all the time. But deep down I was just a fragile young lad who made a huge mistake.

Carly was pregnant with our son when it actually happened,

and he was around one when it came to the sentencing as I say, so that was tough to deal with too. We were a young family and I'd gone and done something stupid which will be with us forever and it wasn't until I went to France when I began to be able to let it go.

That moment on that night was a turning point for the rest of my life and for a long time I probably didn't even like myself and like the way I was as a person because of what I did. For a long while I was miserable, unapproachable and just generally sad in terms of the way I went about my day-to-day business. Once I learned to forgive myself I began to enjoy life again and I feel like I can be myself again nowadays.

If I'm being totally honest, when the enormity of it all hit, I was certain my career was over if I'd been sent down and gone to prison. People were talking about jail quite a lot and although I began to realise that I was young enough to pick my career up after I came out of prison, it was a worrying period for me and it's had such a massive impact on me then, shortly after and forever more. It's the single biggest thing that has happened in my life in terms of the impact it's had on me, without a shadow of a doubt.

But this isn't a sob story, and I don't want to come across asking for sympathy and sounding like I don't deserve what came my way because, believe me, I deserved every single bit of the punishment and the negative spotlight I managed to attract due to what happened on that night. I just feel it's important that if I'm going to tell my story, then I have the right to tell people how it impacted on me, and how doing something - me, not anyone else - so gravely wrong had a profound effect on me and my family the rest of my life.

People may think I'm a dickhead and I held that against myself personally for a long time, but I know that I made a massive error and the fact it took over a decade to get over it and begin to let it go is how seriously I took it.

When it all came to an end and I did manage to avoid jail, the relief was incredible. I didn't have the slightest idea when it came to how I was going to be sentenced or what was going to happen to me right until the words came out of the judge's mouth. I was a nervous wreck stood in that dock and I was thinking about going to prison. Like I say, the bag was under my arm and I'm readying myself to get in that van and get farmed off to jail.

It was a lot of pressure and my actions deserved that pressure, because every action has a consequence. It wasn't easy for a young lad to deal with, especially living in a fishbowl like Bradford at a time where the Bulls were the number one thing in the city and the thing most people could relate to because they were successful. That made the pressure all the more intense. But that's life; you do something wrong, you deal with the consequences.

There were loads of knock-on effects from it. You don't go on BBC or Sky Sports and do punditry, because they look at you in a more negative light. I also lost my Great Britain place. They didn't pick me due to the incident, and it wasn't down to my form, because I was playing in a team that won the treble in 2003. People don't want to associate with the kind of person who has been in the press for doing something like that away from the field, someone without a clean slate. That's what happens when you get into trouble.

I've apologised to his brother for what happened and the amount of trouble I put his whole family through and I certainly don't want them to think I haven't felt guilty for them for years, as Eddie has passed away since the incident took place. I feel like I've said what I needed to say to his brother and it made me feel a little bit at peace with it all, because I just wanted them to know how sorry I was. At the end of the day I was in the wrong and I had to learn to forgive myself. It took a long, long time - and I'll never forget what happened and what I did - but I did manage to forgive myself eventually.

# CHAPTER VII

Even though 2003 was a very iconic year for the Bradford club, it was the most stressful year of my life with the court case going on off the field. I had a full year with the case looming over me, which was due to take place at the end of the year, so basically I was always thinking about what might happen in the back of my mind.

But there were some great times on the field that year as Bradford became the first side in Super League history to win the treble: the League Leaders' Shield, the Challenge Cup and the Grand Final - something I was lucky to do again with St Helens in 2006.

In that Challenge Cup final that year, we were playing against Leeds at Cardiff's Millennium Stadium. I was due to be coming on off the bench as a bit of a utility, as I had been doing for most of that year. I would cover wing, centre, full-back and all that but on the morning of the game, Mick woke up and complained that he had an issue with his groin.

Quite a large part of my life has involved playing Leeds and being in rivalries with Leeds. As a Bradford lad, it's to be expected really. Growing up around Bradford I learned we quickly had a good rivalry with Leeds and when I played against them when I was younger, I learned it even quicker. But they had some players there coming through who were proper Leeds lads like Jamie Jones-Buchanan, Rob Burrow and Danny McGuire and with us having a few Bradford lads in the team, it made the passion between the two sides when we played even greater.

So, suddenly after Mick withdrawing, I'm in the team because they put Robbie back into full-back to replace Mick and I ended up playing in the halves in a cup final. I had been playing a little bit of six that year leading up to the game so I knew I was up to the job, but it was the first game I'd played in a major final in a pivotal role. It was by far the biggest game of my career to that point because I'd not been playing there regularly. Suddenly I'm starting a cup final against our arch-rivals at stand-off. It was nerve-wracking to say the least.

Especially when you don't find out until the morning of the game. I remember Mick saying he wasn't right at all and Nobby hooked me to one side in the hotel and basically said I was in. It was, and still is, the only time before a game where I've been physically sick due to nerves. Normally I'm fine but on that day, the enormity of it was huge. I just couldn't stop thinking how big a game it was. I was telling myself all the time, 'Oh my God, we can't lose to Leeds. We just can't!'

That was my first final against Leeds too, and I knew how much it meant to everyone back home. The game itself is a bit of a blur, but I remember we were properly clinging on towards the back end trying to stay ahead. Jamie Peacock had an absolutely huge game for us. He'd just come back from putting his hand through a window, but he was inspirational on the day. It was one of those games that goes by in a flash.

I remember always wanting to play at Wembley throughout my career, but it had just been knocked down a few years earlier and was being rebuilt. But after Wembley - and getting to play there later in my career - I can honestly say Cardiff and the Millennium Stadium was just behind it in terms of the buzz. When they put the roof on and it created that massive atmosphere, it was like nothing I'd ever heard before.

It was packed to the rafters. The atmosphere was so good that you could literally feel it and the stands are right over the top of you. It's quite imposing as a venue. I remember that we couldn't hear each other out on the field because the crowd were going nuts and it was that loud.

But even though my memory can be patchy, the one thing I will never forget about that day is that it wasn't long after my son, William, had just been born. He must have been about six months old. I remember going to get him from Carly from the side of the pitch and getting him onto the team picture. You're not allowed to do that anymore as you can get a massive fine. That's one thing I'll never forget, having him on the photos, but it was nice to contribute in a big game for once and not just be a bench player.

I felt like I defended well, but I'd class what you'd call a 'good game' as one where I score a couple of tries, or set a few up, or have an impact in attack on the game. I did my part, but it still wasn't enough for me. To be a pivotal part of a team, you've got to be playing consistently on a weekly basis so you can build up form. Repetition is key and when you've been getting moved around it's hard to slot in and be incredible. But it was a good all-round team performance, and that's what Bradford Bulls was about at that time - putting the team first.

Leeds seemed to follow me around through my career, because when I was at St Helens it was Saints-Leeds that became the biggest rivalry in rugby league, and the one that was in the most finals. But I enjoyed it, I enjoyed the healthy competition and the rivalry it brought. It's a little bit like Manchester United and

Liverpool. The big occasions bring the best out of you. I've got massive respect for those players now though. When you're young you're quite hot-headed and you don't care too much for them, but nowadays you look at what Danny and Rob - and Kevin Sinfield - have done, and you can't help but admire them.

You don't hate each other, but you've got a strong dislike for each other when you're on the field. Off the field you don't mix, because it's Bradford versus Leeds. But nowadays I can look back and have a massive amount of respect for what they have all done in their careers - as well as so many other great players I've had battles with who I grew up playing against. They were the best ones to win, the finals against Leeds. But that's me being a proud Bradfordian.

That year all the players also got the opportunity to play for their county at professional level for the first time with the introduction of the Yorkshire v Lancashire games - and they were great. It's amazing it's not been done since and I don't think it was given long enough to build up a proper history and a rivalry. I think the fans liked it too.

I really enjoyed it and I know all the other lads did too from speaking to them. They looked after us really well and it felt like a proper camp. We went off to hotels, trained away and we got proper training gear to go with it even though the game itself was only down the road from where I lived. It was a good break from club rugby and in my opinion they should have stuck with it because they were proper competitive games.

More importantly though, they were games that we'd all experienced as youngsters. When you're going through the ranks as a kid you play for Yorkshire against Lancashire and it's always something you take great pride in, so it made sense to have it at senior level. I remember thinking it was a great move when they brought it in - and I got to play full-back in a game that was actually played at Odsal. It's what you're brought up on, that rivalry, and if they'd given it more time, it might have worked.

So after starting the cup final at stand-off and having a good run in the team at six throughout the year, I ended up finding myself on the bench again for the Grand Final of 2003 against Wigan. To be honest, I think it's just where I was in the pecking order at that time. That's just how it was and I don't hold any grudges about it.

I find it hard to talk about things I hold little relevance to, and that's why Grand Finals like that I don't remember too much about. Don't get me wrong, I remember playing in the final and it was amazing that we won it and we won the treble, but from a personal perspective, I didn't want to just be the guy who ran around without any real influence.

That wasn't who I wanted to be. I was lucky I played in a good team and I didn't contribute loads to it. I did okay. I was proud I was involved with such a great team, but I wanted to be playing better than I did at the time, despite winning the lot that year in 2003.

When I won the treble with Bradford, I was here, there and everywhere. It felt a bit default. In the cup final I was in because someone else had got injured, whereas in 2006 I was a crucial part of the team. I played every week at stand-off and I genuinely contributed, so to me, those memories are stronger. It's huge to win the treble and it was huge for Bradford at the time, but for me, it's hard to get psyched up because we expected it at Bradford.

When you're in a winning process you just tick the Challenge Cup off and target the next one. You don't celebrate for weeks on end. I remember the impact the treble had on the club and the place, but personally, I just felt I could do so much more and it's why it doesn't hold massive amounts of substance with me.

But one thing I'll never forget about the Grand Final was that my good mate Stuart Reardon won the Harry Sunderland Trophy for man of the match. That was huge. I was really proud of him, because he came from absolutely nowhere that season and the club winning it was topped off by him doing that. He scored a brilliant try in the final and he got the recognition he deserved off the back of it, being in the Great Britain team. I thought it was thoroughly deserved. It was the highlight of the whole occasion for me.

The team spirit we had at Bradford at that time was incredible though, and nobody summed that up better than big Lesley Vainikolo, who we signed at the end of 2001. The impact he had on the Bulls as a club was huge, but off the field and in training, he was brilliant.

Things weren't always plain sailing. One time during the glory years at Bradford we'd hit a bit of a sticky run of form, and believe me, Nobby gave it to us one day in training in a session, hammering us about what we were doing wrong. What did we need to change? Les had an idea, standing up and declaring, 'I think we should do some more fitness, coach.' What? Fitness? That's every rugby league player's worst nightmare, extra fitness work! What's he on about?

We're looking at him with a perplexing gaze and it turned out Les knew exactly what he was doing. He wanted some fitness work getting into the players because he was off back to Tonga for a family gathering for a whole fortnight - which nobody knew until we came in to do our fitness and Les wasn't there. What a guy! He's off on a break and we're being hammered with fitness work. Genius!

But it was in 2004 where I'd really started to become a bit more of a stand-off and getting some chances in that position. I played in the World Club Challenge against Penrith at six - with Karl Pratt alongside me in the halves, if I remember correctly. But we both had really good games despite not being considered as out-and-out half-backs and we won what is rightly assumed to be the biggest game in club rugby league. We helped Bradford become champions of the world against a really good team, so with that being before the season had started I thought I was in and I thought I'd get at least a good run at stand-off.

We played Salford in a game at Odsal early on in the season and I wasn't great. I think we only won 25-18, and I don't think too many of us were great that day to be honest. It was an off-day admittedly from a personal perspective, but the next week I got dropped by Nobby. That was the day where it really hit home that I wasn't going to have a future at stand-off at Bradford. If I wanted to achieve what I wanted to do in my brain then I would have to move - and although I didn't do so for another 18 months, that was when I began to realise that my long-term future probably was elsewhere.

We were so tightly knit as a group. We were in each other's pockets all the time and we created a special bond that you can't replicate. Just playing for the Bulls meant everything to me, but as I got more and more frustrated it became quickly apparent that it was time to go.

There was no way I wanted to leave Bradford at that time and the prospect of doing so was unthinkable and pretty gut-wrenching, but at some point, I knew I had to put myself first, given how I was approaching my mid-20s and my supposed peak years. I don't have any issues with Brian Noble and even to this day we still get on, and I will forever respect the job he did in producing Bradford's best ever years, but at that time, I didn't see it working between us both. I'd be bench, full-back, wing, stand-off, then back to the wing.

I can hold my hands up and say that I wasn't the best trainer and I wasn't the ideal role model for some kids coming through because I didn't train hard. I just loved playing. I liked the skills sessions in training, but the fitness and the weights is the thing I hate, and I suspect Nobby perhaps wondered if he thought it was time for us to part ways anyway.

But I wanted to talk at length about Brian really, even though leaving Bradford was really hard and I thought I could have given it a really good shot at six for the Bulls. I would have hoped that they would have tried harder to keep me and fight and scrap as much as St Helens did to make me their player, but it is what it is.

Since saying that though, I've never had a bad relationship with Nobby. He's always been someone I've got along with and he's a really fun bloke and a good guy to be around. At the end of my time at Bradford and me moving on to Saints, it just didn't work out with him, but there is no bad blood there whatsoever. I still get on with him to this day and he was absolutely class with the court case when I was a kid at Bradford.

After everything he did with me through the court case and the support he gave me, he's a great guy to be around and I really enjoyed being around him when I was at Bradford.

Anyway, I had conversations with Nobby throughout the latter part of 2004 and I got the impression as the talks went on that if I wanted to have a fish around and have a look at what's out there when my contract's up, if I wasn't happy, he'd be fine with that.

I'm a bit of a sulker and I suspect I was probably a negative influence in and around training at the time, but that's me. It's who I am. I remember a game against Leeds and he played Robbie Paul and Paul Deacon in the halves. I love Robbie, but we were vying for the same position and I just got the feeling that he was always in front of me.

Midway through that season we signed Iestyn Harris and some people might have felt that said a lot in regards to what direction they wanted to go in moving forward. For me, it said everything. There was no chance of me staying from thereon out in my opinion. I hadn't agreed anything with anyone - I couldn't as I was still under contract - about staying or going by that point, but it was just obvious where my future was: away from Odsal and away from Bradford.

# Robbie Hunter-Paul

## (Bradford Bulls team-mate)

Where do you start when it comes to talking about Leon Pryce?

The first time I ever met him was when I'd been asked to give out the trophies at a Bradford Schools cup final down at Odsal Stadium. I was invited to award the winners with the trophy and Leon was in that team. His cousin Waine was in there too, and Stuart Reardon, to name but a couple.

But it was quite embarrassing to watch because he was so much better than everyone else on that pitch - and I can't overstate that enough. He was that good. He scored three tries in that final and it was like a man against boys. He destroyed everyone, threw them all over the field with his freakish strength he had at that age. Then once he'd got his three, he turned into a provider.

He was running into the in-goal area after breaking down the field and waited for a team-mate to catch up with him so that they could get a try to their name too. He was head and shoulders above the competition and you knew then that this kid was destined for the very top. From the beginning you could see he was something special.

I've grown up with a lot of gifted and talented athletes in my career and life, but I'd never come across someone at that age who was that good. When he joined the Bulls as a 15-year-old, I'd never seen his equal - and I spent some time with some great players growing up. Players like Stacey Jones, Joe Vagana, my own brother, Henry Paul, but Leon was so gifted at that time in comparison.

He had the luxury of maturing early in his career, so physically he was more mature than his peers of the same age group, which allowed him to climb the ranks quicker. But we were all astonished. He was earmarked for a massive future and he was a game-breaker from an early age. He was tipped up as international class from a young age and he didn't disappoint in that regard. His ability was astonishing.

It was disappointing from my point of view that even though we left the same year, it was sad to see him leave Bradford at the end of 2005, because I knew just how much more there was to come from him. I also knew how he lived, breathed and ate Bradford - the club was coursing through his veins and he loved the place. It was heartbreaking to see him leave and he's always identified Bradford as his club and even though he's been so successful at St Helens, Catalans and Hull, he would still refer to Bradford as 'us'.

That's what made it so disappointing. I was coming to the back end of my career, but I was really close with him and I understood that it was his time to lead this club when I went. I think it's something he always wanted to do but at the same time, he went away from his comfort zone and he had to put his head above the parapet and test himself somewhere else, which was great to see him do.

He is just a talented man. Going to Saints was great in hindsight because he developed a new life and a new way of playing which took him to a whole other level. I'm not sure he thought that the coaching structure that was in place at the Bulls at that time had the faith in him or vice-versa. I wasn't directly involved in that relationship, but I think he felt he needed to step into the unknown.

But it was a smart move for his career - although someone who's a Bulls fan like I am, it was still heartbreaking to see him walk out of the door and fulfil his potential somewhere else. I think there was an opportunity missed for the Bulls there. But Saints brought the best out of him and it made him hungrier than ever. In the long run it maybe wasn't the best thing to ever happen to Bradford, but it was the best thing to happen to him.

As for Leon the person, it's pretty much the same thing: I saw this young, talented athlete who looked up to me - and that was something new to me. I was only 18 at the time I first met him and it was amazing to be idolised. I guess we gravitated towards each other a little because we were on the younger end of the spectrum and we hung out together a lot.

I saw him as a bit of a younger brother. He used to ask me for advice and I felt responsible to look out for him. You're influenced by your peers and his personality is shaped by those of us who were intimately close to him. You like to hope you did right by him. Some things I'm really proud of and some I'm not in that regard! I nurtured him and we became really close.

As players at the Bulls, we had a little bit of a clique going on and Leon was just coming into his own as a young man and a young professional and he was getting influenced by some of the biggest names in the sport. I always found the time to talk to Leon and make sure he was all good.

There were some synergies he saw in the way I was as a person and the way potentially he aspired to be a bit like me. We'd have a few beers, pull each other aside and cry on each other's shoulders. We could always speak to each other openly - just like you would with a family member. We call each other brothers. I've always had Henry, but I've not had a vast array of colleagues I've been able to share everything with. He's seen me at my best and my worst - and vice-versa. We don't judge each other, we're always there for one another and I would never leave him on his own.

I'd like to think I'd been there for Leon and he's been there for me without question. The machoism and masculinity surrounding our job quickly fell away and we became in touch with each other as people - that's what grew our bond. He gave me one of the biggest accolades of my life - and I've lifted every trophy going - when he asked me to be the godfather to his son, William.

It shocked me, it really did. But it made me immensely proud. To see the beautiful young person William has turned into, it shows what a wonderful job he and Carly have done as parents and as people. Those kids are testament to the true love that comes between those two guys.

I knew Carly before I knew Leon. She worked up at the Bulls before Leon broke through so I know them both and I know and love their family very deeply. It's been an amazing journey with me and the Pryces. He's got a really good heart individually and when people were being hurt around him like the crisis at the Bulls in 2016, he personally carried that group of young men. I could see the pain in his eyes and he protected them very well - he's a wonderful human being.

That's all I can say about him. He's the opposite of selfish. He's got a giant heart and he cares about people so much.

But don't mug him off - he'll give you a slap!

# CHAPTER VIII

I think it's been made pretty clear that by now, I didn't want to go anywhere else. I made it quite obvious in the press and the things I was saying that at that time, before I finished up at Bradford, I just didn't want to leave the club and move on, even if it turned out to be the right decision in the long run.

*From Bradford Telegraph and Argus, 14th March 2005: "I've got until December left on my contract and I just want to get one position locked down and really work at it," Pryce said. "There are no dramas with me. Hopefully it will be sorted in the near future. I love Bradford and as long as we can sort a few things out there will be no problems."*

Anyway, once I'd decided I wanted to have a look around and see what was available for 2006 there were options appearing quite quickly, which was nice to see. There were rumours linking me with rugby union, although there wasn't too much in that - but that would materialise later in my career. However, the two main clubs that were interested straight away were both Super League teams: St Helens and Wigan.

That may sound like a tough decision to make, but as soon as St Helens made their interest formal I was leaning towards them quite quickly. Lee Gilmour had signed there already and he was someone I knew quite well, and Nick Fozzard and Paul Anderson both travelled across from Yorkshire too, which was beneficial. Once I'd spoken to Daniel Anderson and looked at that team, I had to figure out what would work best for me. The kind of player I am, I know that first of all, the likes of Paul Sculthorpe and Paul Wellens - who I knew from Great Britain camps I'd been on - were exceptional players and they would help take me to the next level.

Gilly was someone else who I looked at and thought I could do something similar to him. At Bradford he was a gap-filler like myself, but when he went to Saints he would go on and play in a regular position.

He was putting a good word in for me at St Helens with the players and the coaches too and that helped, I think. He was only 25 or 26 at that time - a year or two older than me - and he would go on and become world-class in my opinion.

Pretty early on I'd decided that with a young family with my son, William, just being born and everyone around me at home, I wouldn't be leaving Bradford to move somewhere else, irrespective of the offers coming in.

I had to decide what I wanted to do with that in mind, but once I looked at that St Helens team, I knew that if I was going to fulfil my potential of being a stand-off who could play at any level, I'd need to play with a scrum-half like Sean Long. I knew that there were some guys travelling already too in Baloo, Gilly and Foz, and that pretty much swayed me, if I'm being honest.

Elsewhere, there were plenty of other lads who slowly revealed to each other that they'd decided it was time to move on, too. It was bizarre that it was all somehow happening at once. It was like the heart was being ripped out of the Bulls. Stuart Reardon got offered a really good contract by Warrington, but he didn't want to go. However, the money they were offering him, he couldn't really turn it down, and I don't think anyone held it against him because he had to do what was right for him and his career at that time.

Lee Radford had agreed to go back home and go and play for Hull FC, Jamie Peacock had agreed to go to Leeds, I was leaving because I'd penned my deal to sign for St Helens, Rob Parker was going to Salford and Robbie Paul was going to Huddersfield, so it was all coming to an end in a strange, strange way, with so many leaving at the same time.

The contract talks with St Helens were informally sorted midway through the year, as I couldn't sign until later and who knows, when all the lads like myself, JP and Radders got their futures sorted, perhaps that was another thing that helped us come together and play our best stuff at exactly the right time.

However, when the deal was agreed at Saints for 2006 and I knew I could concentrate on rugby, my form picked up without a shadow of a doubt. I started getting played regularly in one position - I was on the right wing, I think - and that also helped.

From there, things just got better and better as that season rolled on. It was like, 'I know where I am now, I know what I'm doing; let's all make sure we go out on a real high at Odsal.' Bradford fans will look back and be sad that all those players left at the same time because it changed the course of the club's history, but in reality, we were galvanised and determined to go out on a high.

I'd like to think that I understand the game really well and at that time, I could cover a load of different positions which when you're 18 or 19 and looking to get into the team any way possible, is great. But when you were at the age I was at - coming into my mid-20s - I knew what my best position was and where I wanted to play.

I didn't want to be a gap-filler anymore, I wanted to be a half-back or at least someone who was playing in the same spot each and every week, and in the run-in to winning at Old Trafford in 2005 I was on the wing every week, and that was at least helping me hit some decent form and be in good nick.

On the whole, 2005 was a strange year, perhaps the strangest I've known during my time in the sport. We were having a really poor season up until midway through the year. We got knocked out of the Challenge Cup by Hull, and we weren't doing too great in the league. Obviously we knew things were happening behind the scenes. Whether that impacted on our season, I don't know. I think it might have done because as I say, when it was done and dusted and everyone finalised their plans for 2006, it all clicked.

I vividly remember a day at training where we all sat down, the lads who were leaving, and had a bit of a head-to-head with each other. We all said that we were moving on and leaving the Bulls, we all love each other's company and we loved each other as teammates, so let's go out there and just do it for each other one last time before we all start new chapters. That galvanised us I think, that one meeting we had, because before that our season was going nowhere.

We had a day out drinking where we all went out on the beer in fancy dress and that day massively summed up what the Bulls were great at. We were all like a family, out together and having fun. It was a turning point in our season too, as strange as it sounds.

That was the day that changed us as a team because we came together after that and we became a proper unit. From thereon out I think we went 12 games unbeaten to win Super League, and as well as the existing group we already had, the club made a really smart move in bringing Ian Henderson in to give us an extra bit of zip.

At first though, I remember looking at Hendo in training. Admittedly he'd only just got off the plane and he looked a little bit off the pace and I wasn't sure what to think of him. How wrong was I! By the time he'd settled in, he began to rip the competition and our opponents to bits, and he was just killing it. We've actually stayed friends since and we played together at Catalans. He's a top bloke and he made a difference that year to us. He's a tight bastard who doesn't like spending his money, but a great bloke nonetheless!

Just before I left I made a reference to the fact the club had signed some older players for 2006 in the Telegraph and Argus:

*From Bradford Telegraph and Argus, 1st October 2005: "I'm only 23, I've got plenty of time and hopefully I'll be back here one day to finish my career off. With the aged signings we are making at the moment, you can't rule out me coming back here at 32!"*

Looking back, I'm crazy for saying stuff like that, but that's me all over. Nobody would say that in the week leading up to a Grand Final, would they! But on the field, I wanted to nail down one role and that was a big part of why it probably ended so well, I reckon.

St Helens made me feel really wanted - especially Eamonn McManus - and the decision to tell Bradford was actually a lot easier than people would have guessed. It was all done and dusted pretty quickly and, in truth, it wasn't necessarily the club in general, but when you sign Iestyn Harris to come in and play stand-off, it sends a pretty clear message out about what the club's intentions for you are in my opinion. That's nothing against Iestyn, of course. It was just business and I get on very well with Iestyn and he's helped me out with my career since then.

I met Eamonn and Daniel Anderson the day after having a game against St Helens midway through that year, funnily enough - the one where I almost knocked Jamie Lyon's head off and got a red card for it, so I didn't think I was going to be too popular heading into that meeting!

I had already been to see Wigan as it turned out, because Ian Millward tried to get me to go there after he left St Helens, so they were definitely keen. But Ian was particularly interested because he'd tried to sign me for Saints in the past. Him leaving St Helens obviously made me wonder if I was going to get the move there and whether I should look at Wigan as a serious option, so I went to meet Ian and Wigan before heading over to meet St Helens. I didn't realise it then, but looking back, it was massive to know that both clubs wanted to sign me.

Daniel Anderson had just turned up at St Helens and I went and met both he and the chairman at a TGI Fridays in Bury, just off the motorway. I went in saying, 'I'm so sorry for what I did to Jamie Lyon,' and they just both blew up laughing. 'Don't be so stupid,' Eamonn said, and that settled me down and instantly made me feel comfortable around them both. I guess they could have taken it much worse if they'd wanted to!

I knew I could be a much better player at another club than I was at Bradford, and I wanted to prove it to Saints that we were the right fit for each other. I admitted to them I felt I could take my game to a level I hadn't yet hit by becoming a permanent stand-off, and do you know what, it just felt like they were really receptive to what I had to say and, more importantly than anything, they just listened to me.

I told them I could become an international player, win major trophies as a key part of a team and I had the desire to do it - and if it meant leaving Bradford, so be it. I didn't want to leave, but I had to go and prove myself at the highest level. By the time I left that restaurant, the vibe I was getting from Daniel was incredibly positive - although I hadn't signed by that point, as I couldn't due to the timing of the meeting. You couldn't sign deals with clubs when you were coming off contract until a certain point of the year. I think it's May these days, but back then it was a lot later than that.

I spoke to my old man and Robbie about it and in all honesty I just didn't know what to do when it came down to actually signing. I'd confided in people about something that was such a difficult decision, because I really didn't want to leave and I really didn't want to join St Helens, but I woke up one morning and just thought, 'Sod it, I'm off'.

Looking back, it was the single best decision I've ever made in my life - bar none. At the time it was a massive head-blag, though. You have moments in your life and decisions you can make that you learn from if they're wrong, and at the time I thought it was a horrendous situation to be in.

So with that done and dusted - I'm off to St Helens - it was time to worry about the present. I immediately got my head switched onto winning something with Bradford one last time and If I'm being honest, we never felt like we were going to lose on the run-in to Old Trafford at all - and even if we did come close on one or two occasions, we just collectively knew we would beat teams. That's a special feeling to have and something I've only experienced a handful of times, although maybe I'm lucky to have tasted that as often as I did.

That Grand Final was a pretty important one for so many reasons. We were all leaving, but for the Bradford lads, the fact it was against Leeds and they'd beaten us the year before upped the stakes a little in our eyes. I didn't play in the 2004 Grand Final because I was injured - I'd done my shoulder just before it - but it was so emotional really, like nothing I'd ever experienced up to that point.

The week running up to the game, we'd done all the usual stuff, like the photos and the interviews before, but this was different. It was quite sad in a way, because I wanted to go out with a bang, but the way it ended, I could have never believed it. The team spirit I've spoken about so much was pivotal; I don't think it swung the match or the title in our favour, but it helped for sure.

And even though a few of us were leaving, there was still time for one big moment from a very big character in Lesley Vainikolo. In our last training session before the Grand Final in 2005 - we'd done a few hits on the tackling shield and we naturally got ourselves all fired up - we fell into a big circle and had one last briefing from the coach before we went and did our own preparation for the big game. Now these sessions are like no other, so we were all focussed on what Nobby would say to us before we went off home. Well, everyone except Les.

Nobby was facing us all and he was telling us what would win us the game, what would give us the trophy, and he was hammering on about defence and everything like that. It was good stuff, it really was. Nobby knew how to motivate us before a big game, it was part of what made him such a good coach.

He was really getting us pumped up, but Les, who was stood just behind him and probably just out of his eyeline, was sensing an opportunity to get one over on him. Off guard, just as Nobby finished doing his big inspirational team talk, I saw Les out of the corner of my eye duck down into a spear-like position and start to charge into the coach!

It was literally like life in slow motion, so I dread to think what it was like for Nobby himself! He smashed him with his shoulder, Nobby's head whiplashed back and he slammed onto the floor with a real thud. It was hilarious, although it looked bad at the time. But I guess that's what it was like to be slammed by The Volcano, the living legend that is Lesley Vainikolo. I wish I could relive that moment because it was really, really funny and everyone was in hysterics.

Anyway, after smashing him, Les just screams at him, 'No coach! That's what's going to win us the game!' while standing over him and pointing in his face. Nobby's face was completely startled, because he'd almost been knocked unconscious by one of his own players and I'm not sure he really knew what planet he was on at that point. He was looking up at Lesley and trying to find the words to say something back, but he had nearly been knocked out - the poor bloke! We're all looking at each other and aren't sure whether to laugh or run for the hills, because as soon as Nobby came to his senses, he was going to have Lesley.

Eventually the whole group just erupted and that was typical of the kind of banter and spirit we had at Bradford. Only Les could have gotten away with that. I think if anyone else had done it the day before a Grand Final they would have been dropped - but you couldn't drop the big man, could you! Nobby was great with the way he dealt with it - when he properly came round, that is - and the look on his face when he was staring up at Les stood over him pointing at him is something I'll genuinely never forget. I'd pay to see that again, I really would. Like I say, I wish I could go back and relive that moment because it was so funny - and Nobby took it really well to be fair to him!

But those big games tend to all become a bit of a blur for me looking back, because you're so focussed on the match to worry about what's happening, but the try I scored that night really does stick out in my mind. I got the ball and looked left to pass and just broke away. But for some crazy reason, which I still don't understand to this day, the ball popped out of my hand as I was running free in broken field. It was another one of those moments where life turned into slow motion. The ball slowly wormed its way out of my grasp as I broke away and I remember thinking, 'Shit, I'm going to drop this!'

Somehow, I kept hold of it and dived over the line. The emotion just escaped me in a way I've never known before. I'd managed to do something significant in a big game and a final. I was so happy I could round off my last game for Bradford with a try and a big win.

On the night, we played really well and we did everything right, nothing too out of the ordinary and ticked all the boxes to perfection. By that point we had started winning games consistently and we knew what we had to do to win. In big games like that, the team who are chasing generally seem to lose. You don't often get teams coming from behind to win because you end up over-panicking and overdoing the things you're used to doing. Paul Deacon wore them down with his kicking.

So there you have it, we've done it. We've gone out on a high and actually won the Grand Final against Leeds and boy, did we celebrate. We drank all the way through the night on the Saturday, given how it was our last real game together, and then we had the parade the day after with the trophy, and hardly any of us had slept. We'd gone through for over 24 hours. At Odsal there was an old press room up in the white terrapins. Anyone who has been to the ground in recent years will know it. But while the press used it on match days, we actually used it to have a drink and a social occasion in from time to time.

We'd got in there and we'd had a few bottles of beer and the banter was flowing - with some of the guys well on their way to being pretty smashed, I've got to be honest. Anyway, the door opened at one point which caught us all a bit by surprise and it was a young lad from the press. I can't remember his name. He was walking in at a time where nobody was allowed in, because it was players only on that particular day. Les was pretty pissed by this point and from nowhere, like he had a couple of days earlier with Nobby, dipped his shoulder and smacked his full body into this poor young kid who really didn't suspect it.

Now with Nobby, it was a bit more of a laugh because it was on a grassy field and the coach knew how to take a hit, even if it was from a big wrecking ball like Lesley Vainikolo. But Les had cleaned through this kid and he'd missed a table by literally millimetres before landing head first onto the carpet. I can't remember what Les said exactly when he stood over him, but we went into meltdown this time because we were fearing the worst. Essentially this was Les tackling a member of the public. Thankfully, the press kid took it really well. So we picked him up, dusted him down, apologised and sent him on his way. Anything that Les does is in good jest and with good humour and he'd never intentionally hurt anyone, it was just for a bit of fun - and anyone who knows him will know that.

So we quickly get back into the drinking and the celebrations, but five minutes later an old guy comes walking around the corner and into the room we were all in. Again, it was strictly players only. I'm not sure if it was another member of the press, but he walked in, and straight away a few of us pre-empted it this time and we had a feeling what Les would do, so we all rapidly turned to Les only to see him getting ready to drop the shoulder again. 'Jesus Christ', we're all thinking. 'Don't do it, Les!'

This guy was old - I think he was about 70 - and we all had to dive on Les to stop him doing the worst, because if this guy had been hit by The Volcano, that was probably it - he was dead! Thank God we managed to stop him in time, although I remember it took a few of us to jump on top of him to stop him. That was Les though: unpredictable, hilarious and just a brilliant guy to have around the place. He was awesome. The story I've told in another chapter, about him getting the players in for fitness when he was off on holiday to Tonga for a fortnight, was typical Les.

So that was it, the end of an era, I guess. But at the time I really didn't think it was the end, in many ways, because I didn't envisage the Bulls would fall as far as they did, despite all the players that were leaving. I don't think anyone could have foreseen that, could they?

I thought the Bulls would always be up there and if that was the case it wasn't the end of anything really, it was just a few players moving on - life goes on for the club. It felt strange the day after because, bang, that was it, I wasn't a Bradford player anymore. It's all I'd ever known and I found it very hard to leave and get used to the fact I wasn't training in Bradford initially. It was seriously tough to deal with mentally.

With so many players leaving there were a lot of goodbyes, but I think one of the departures could have been managed a lot better - and that was Robbie's. I don't think it was done the right way, if I'm being honest.

I just think it could have been handled a little bit better. He had been such an iconic player for the club since he arrived. He was up there with the likes of Keith Mumby and Trevor Foster in Bradford's history and he had been allowed to leave without being made a fuss of.

I tried to say that on the microphone in 2005 when we had a big trophy parade at Odsal, that we needed to deflect the attention onto Robbie. With all due respect to everyone else, the service Robbie had given that club and the work he had done both on and - more importantly - off the field was huge. I wanted them to appreciate Robbie's service and what he had done for Bradford.

And when I started to turn my head to the new job and try to move on from Bradford, I honestly didn't realise how big a club St Helens were. Throughout my time negotiating with them to go there I wasn't ever completely sure because it meant I was leaving Bradford, but when I got there it was very, very different. It hit me very quickly how serious the place was - and that's nothing against Bradford - but instantly I got the feel it was a very good place and it was going to be a good move.

Turns out it was even better than that - it was bloody brilliant.

# CHAPTER IX

I guess you always feel a bit strange going into a new club, but the whole town and the whole St Helens club just made it, well ... easy. That might sound a bit cocky and arrogant, but what I mean by that is that I looked around and realised I was playing in a team that had Keiron Cunningham, Sean Long, Paul Wellens, Paul Sculthorpe, Jamie Lyon ... I could go on and on. It was stacked full of talent there at the time.

You suddenly feel like there's less pressure on you because you aren't going to be overly relied on too much. When you're leaving two internationals out like Nick Fozzard and Vinnie Anderson in the Grand Final in my first year there in 2006, you start to realise how crazily good that team was and how much it was a once-in-a-generation thing. It's the greatest team ever to play in Super League history, without a shadow of a doubt. There's no questioning that fact in my eyes.

It would be easy for me to sit and talk through all of that team because essentially, almost all of them were internationals. But in my opinion, Super League will never see a player the like of Jamie Lyon ever again, so I have to mention him at some length.

When I took Jamie out and got sent off for it the year earlier while I was still playing at Bradford, I didn't realise at the time that I'd end up at St Helens a few months later - and Jamie didn't speak to me for a long time, a good few months! He clearly wasn't happy with me, and it turned out I had to apologise to him for the tackle to put it right. We were on a pre-season training camp and I buttered him up by saying that tackling him the way I did - nearly taking his head off - was the only way I could stop him.

He'd been playing country rugby out in the sticks for Wee Waa, so he came in funny circumstances, but he was just unbelievable. When he started playing, blimey, you couldn't believe the things he could do with that ball. He could get a ball in his hand and whip around any player in the whole competition. His speed was incredible, his acceleration was frightening and his awareness of the game was superb. He's just an all-round completely ridiculous player. You won't come across many players like him in this country - he's gifted. He was born special.

Then there's the coach. Daniel Anderson has had the biggest impact on my career without a shadow of a doubt, bar none. I'm a pretty cocky guy and a confident person, but I absolutely feared him. He was one of only two people I was afraid of in my career alongside my father, and that is genuinely true.

My first game back at Bradford summed up the fear I had for Daniel to perfection. It was obviously a big day for me going back 'home', and fair play to them, they obviously had a plan to work me out and knacker up my grand return. Terry Newton had started spotting me up, which in rugby terms means they were running at me to tire me out over and over again. I wasn't fit enough to cope with that at the time. I was about six or seven kilos overweight and I was gassed!

Daniel hooked me after about 25 minutes. I had to walk all the way around in front of the main stand at Odsal, with tens of thousands of people heckling me and booing me and it was just awful. They'd executed their plan on me to perfection because fitness-wise, I just wasn't right at that point. I was absolutely knackered. I don't think I've ever been as tired in my entire life. At full-time we're all sat in the away sheds at Odsal, and in front of the full team he tore into me in front of everyone. I'll never forget it. He absolutely roasted me. It's the biggest grilling I've ever had.

'You,' he screamed. 'Don't you fucking fire up at full-time or near the end of the game, you do it from the first fucking tackle and make your tackles from the start, you pussy! You're here to supposedly get into the opposition, but you played fucking soft, absolutely soft!'

He was belittling me in front of all these great international players and it was the first time I've ever had strips ripped off me by a coach. But that put me in my place and I remember being sat there feeling embarrassed - he broke me really - but in the long run, I respected Daniel because of it and it taught me to change my game. I probably thought that being a half-back, I just had to turn up and attack, but that made me focus on my defensive performances more and it made me the player I was at my peak.

But that day at Bradford, he tore me a new one - I wasn't the first, and I definitely wouldn't be the last! He was the boss, and he sure as hell made me know that was the case. I was nearly in tears, I genuinely mean that. When I have a little bit of fear for someone I have total respect for them and from then on, and given how I knew his coaching was so good, I had the utmost respect for him and I still do to this very day. If it wasn't for his guidance and his support through a transitional time in becoming a first-choice stand-off for a top club, I would never have been the player I became. I played my best rugby under him and that was no coincidence. He never ripped into me again and that's because I knew I didn't want to incur his wrath. It was like when you get a ticking off from your parents, you don't want to get in trouble again.

The way I play is often talked about by pundits, experts, fans and people like that, but my style is my style and Daniel knew that straight away. I don't think he'd have signed me otherwise.

I know people get frustrated with the fact that I come in and out of games, but I'm not the type of player who is in the thick of it for 80 minutes - and Daniel respected that and that's how he got the best out of me. He knew that if I had a quiet first half he could tap me on the shoulder in the sheds at half-time and say, 'I need you here, mate.'

He understood how he played and more often than not, I would respond. He could manage people to perfection. He would scream at his forwards like Maurie Fa'asavalu and Nick Fozzard, but all he needed to do was whisper in my ear at half-time and tell me it was time to play, and because he knew I respected his methods, that was all that he had to do. I would play for him as well as St Helens and that's the biggest compliment I think I could pay him. He's the number one coach I've had, without a doubt.

Part of the amazing team spirit we had at Saints was built around the fact we weren't afraid to ridicule each other from time to time. Quite a few of the lads were young, single blokes and in all honesty, in and around St Helens they were like celebrities. So if they had a few drinks on a weekend they would always have stories to tell. So we introduced the Goose Award, where we would tell a story which we think could draw the most laughter out of the lads - but mostly it was about each other though!

I got Keiron Cunningham good once, I'll never forget it. We were big rivals with Leeds around that time and Tony Smith was their coach. It was probably the biggest rivalry in the sport in this country. Keiron had spoken in the programme leading up to one of our games about how he thought Tony Smith was a really good coach and he was a big fan of his, so I thought I'd get him good and proper.

One Monday morning when it was time to share stories, I thought I'd have a go for the Goose Award, so I stood up in front of the team and read out what Keiron said in the programme and threw it on the floor in disgust, calling him all the names under the sun. Needless to say, he won the Goose Award that particular week after being slated by all of the lads for 'praising' our big rivals and their coach!

If anyone knows me they know that I play my best rugby when I feel like I've got a little bit of love from the crowd. And from day one at St Helens I had that and I felt like they really appreciated who I was, where I'd come from and what I could bring to them as a team. It was the best six years of my life and I love St Helens. They're just as much my club as Bradford are in a lot of ways.

'Na na na na na na na, Leon Leon Pryce, Leon Pryce, Leon Leon Pryce! Na na na na na na na!' I'll never forget the first time I heard that chant ring out around Knowsley Road. What a buzz that was. I love the Saints fans, I can't emphasise that enough. They're all fantastic. They adopted me as one of their own and I truly felt blessed.

Bradford against Leeds was always big because I'm from

Bradford, and I've always had a friendly rivalry with Leeds which seemed to bring the best out of me. But in my opinion, St Helens versus Wigan was undoubtedly the bigger derby to play in.

I didn't know a great deal about it going into it - I went in a bit blind, I guess - but for any neutral reading this, I can't stress enough how big a deal it is for the people of St Helens and Wigan. Rugby is everything for them, it's like life or death. Saints against Wigan is big because they've always been teams that have been at the top, whereas Bradford's and Leeds' histories have seen peaks and troughs. So I can't put it into words what it was like to play in that derby for the first time in 2006. It blew me away, completely blew me away.

But on the whole, we just didn't feel like we were going to lose that season. We were a stupidly good team. The team spirit was good, but it was so dynamic and so diverse. It was a ridiculously good mixture.

You had the lads from Lancashire who were all young and hung around with each other. There was the Yorkshire Bus - me, Gilmour, Fozzard and Baloo - who were really close, but we integrated well with them and it just worked. You had people at the peak of their careers like Paul Wellens, Sean Long and Keiron Cunningham - who all had a good few years ahead of them - and that mixed with James Graham and James Roby, who were future legends of the game. The imports like Francis Meli, Willie Talau and Jamie Lyon, all settled straight away and became pivotal parts of the team - it was the perfect blend.

I probably loved Bradford so much that I didn't really look at that team and realise how good it was. But from being there just a couple of days, I got the vibe that it was a place that was going to be special to be at and a great group to be involved in. You get narrow-minded when you play for one team for so long and you think you're the best - and I think that was how I felt at Bradford.

As good as we were that year, I remember that the Grand Final was probably - and this is no disrespect to Hull whatsoever, because they had a great team - closer than I imagined it would be early on. However, I scored just before half-time and that was probably a defining moment in the game and it got us over the line. Overall, I thought it was no less than what we deserved. Then it's time for the party, having done what only Bradford had done in the Super League era up until that point: won the lot in one season. Jesus, that was a good night - and the days after it were pretty wild too!

Here's what I remember about it. We've won the Grand Final and as is tradition with Saints, all the families went back to Knowsley Road and had a real good knees-up, which was par for the course at the club anyway!

I recall that it was a really good night and most of the time, while I was playing at Saints, we used to go back to a place called The Griffin Hotel and have a few drinks afterwards. That's where it really got interesting. Jammer, James Graham, had been drinking most of the Saturday night through into Sunday morning, the day after the Grand Final, and he hadn't had much sleep at all. I think him and Lee Gilmour used to throw plenty of banter at each other all the time and it was always going to get out of hand at one point, and this was the occasion - 24 hours after winning the Grand Final!

Anyway, Jammer wanted to borrow Gilly's room key to go upstairs and lay his head down for a bit and have a rest, because we still had plenty of drinking ahead of us - so Lee gave him it, and off he went.

But when he's upstairs asleep, Gilly goes up and looks on Jammer to make sure he's alright, sees that he's dead to the world and decides to come up with a bit of a plan to stitch him up. He told me and Nick Fozzard he was going to dye his hair black in a bid to finally get one up on him - bearing in mind Jammer is as ginger as they come! None of us were going to talk him out of it, so off he goes, in a taxi to Tesco to try and find some hair dye.

He comes back with loads of the stuff, PERMANENT black dye, and he comes up to the room and there's me, Foz and Gilly all stood over a knocked-out Jammer, wondering if we're actually going to do this, because we know he'll go wild. We're giggling away like schoolchildren trying not to wake him up, but to be fair, there was no chance of that with the state Jammer had been in - he was wrecked!

So given how he wanted to do it, he pressed on, laying this thick black hair dye all over Jammer's ginger locks. We also dyed his eyebrows too and for anyone who's seen the film American Pie, he looked like Jim's dad with the two big black caterpillars for eyebrows.

He doesn't move all the way throughout because he's absolutely dead to the world, and as Gilly's rubbing it in, it starts running down his forehead and into his eyes - shit. We knew we couldn't let things go that far because we knew it could do some damage if it got really bad, so we woke him up -

Me and my Grandma when I was a baby!

Me and my mum, Janet - again, very young!

So cute!

Me and our Karl as cute kids!

So young and innocent!

Playing with Queensbury ARLFC as a kid...

...and again winning a trophy!

Me and Karl during our school days!

Me and Karl on the playing fields near our childhood home with our old dog, Bess.

The Pryce family at my mum and dad's wedding.

A non-rugby one: the
day I met Mike Tyson!

With the Bulls' legendary kit-man, Freddy Robinson.

Me - complete with double-denim - getting my shirt from Brian Noble.

Sporting the local attire after winning the Challenge Cup in Edinburgh!
(Dave Williams RLPHOTOS.com)

Me and my old man, Denis...

...and again a few years later - this time with the Challenge Cup.

Champions! After winning the 2003 Challenge Cup in Cardiff.
(Dave Williams RLPHOTOS.com)

With the 2004 World Club Challenge trophy. (Dave Williams RLPHOTOS.com)

I've got plenty of photos with the Challenge Cup!
Here's another; me and William.

Father and son in
matching Bradford
shirts.

What a way to bow out; winning the man of the match in my last game for Bradford, the 2005 Grand Final. (Dave Williams RLPHOTOS.com)

...and with William. (Dave Williams RLPHOTOS.com)

Making sure
William is ready
to play!

Me and Karl
looking proud with
our granddad,
Syd.

On the infamous 2006 tour with Great Britain for the Tri-Nations.
(Dave Williams RLPHOTOS.com)

we had to push him really hard to do it mind! - and told him he had to get in the shower pronto to wash this stuff off of his face.

'Hurry up Jammer,' we're shouting. 'You need to get in the shower mate!' All the while, Jammer is just mumbling as three of us are dragging him to the shower before he gets it all in his eyes.

We drag him into the shower and he's still half-asleep, and we're washing this stuff off of his face for him. I started to feel bad at this point - but probably because I knew what was coming next! He eventually starts to come round as the shower water hits him and he looks in the mirror and sees that his hair has started to turn black! Now, Jammer being Jammer, he didn't take this well at all, so he gets angry and goes mad within a matter of seconds, punches the wall and then punches the window frame too, going berserk.

We tried to get him to calm down, but he was absolutely seething. I didn't know at the time, but that incident where he hit the window frame actually broke his hand, which I think ruled him out of the 2006 Great Britain tour that he'd been selected for. We've all felt guilty for years because of that, to be fair.

Anyway, just after it happened, we tried to stop him, but he got himself off down to the local supermarket and what does he buy? A can of petrol. He rings me up and says something along the lines of, 'I'm going to blow your Yorkshire Bus up!' - which has us in hysterics, and that's not the best idea when Jammer is raging! I remember him on the phone just sounding more and more infuriated by it all as the conversation went on.

He comes back to The Griffin in a fit of rage and threatens to blow my car - the Yorkshire Bus - up again, as well as saying he wants to fight us all in the process. We all nearly end up scrapping in the street trying to calm him down and stop him from doing something ridiculous, trying to remind him that it's just a joke. But his head had completely gone! We left to go and meet the rest of the team at another pub in St Helens and Jammer went off his separate way.

Thank Christ, eventually he settles down and storms off. Phew. That's the end of it we think. But later in the day on the Sunday, we're still drinking and celebrating the Grand Final win and Jammer goes missing again after briefly turning back up. This was in the years before Jammer is earning his millions in Australia, so he's driving a clapped-out little Ford Fiesta at this point. We're all sat outside a pub having a drink and celebrating and he pulls up outside. The car actually had Isle of Man registration plates on and he had to go there to get it. That's how clapped-out it was!

It was like a scene out of EastEnders. He starts revving up his engine and looking at us through the windscreen, and we're all laughing at him because by this point, his hair has gone properly black. He revs his car up, goes to set off to drive into the Yorkshire Bus, and probably the worst thing that could happen to him happened - he stalled the bloody car! That sends us into delirium, so he gets the car going again and actually tries to drive at us, coming up onto the kerb! He missed us by a whisker and we had to dive out of the way of his car, before he drove around the corner of the pub and all I could hear was this thud - I knew he'd driven into the Yorkshire Bus, the car we all use to get across the M62 and get to training. Shit!

We all steam around the back fearing the worst and he's driven into it true to form, as he promised. It took Daniel Anderson to calm him down, as he was in the boozer with us! But it actually turned out that he'd pretty much written off his own car and my big old Picasso - the world-famous Yorkshire Bus - had survived pretty much unscathed!

The way it used to work was we'd have a day of celebrations after the Grand Final on the Sunday and then on the Monday, we'd just keep going right through - it was our 'Mad Monday'. On the Monday he shows up with his black hair and, believe it or not, he'd tried to dye his hair back on the Sunday night to ginger, but it had gone a funny shade of brown! He sat there not speaking to us. I don't think he spoke to me properly for a good six months after that! I think he forgave me in the end, though, because we're really good mates now. We've had a good relationship ever since.

On the field, away from all the mad antics off it, I spoke about how I wanted to go to Saints and link up with Sean Long - and me playing with Longy changed my career. Because I was very athletic I've always been the kind of player to take the ball on. I'm skilful, but I'm not a guy who controls the game. I'm someone who floats in and out of it, so if I could pop into the line where I wanted, it would work.

Keiron Cunningham controlled the forwards, Longy controlled the backs and when he knew it was time for me to come into the game he'd give me the nod, and it was a combination that worked almost straight away. With Longy being so dominant it enabled me to play how I always wanted to play.

When I signed for Saints, I knew from the off that I didn't really want to move my children and my family out of Bradford. My son was settled at school and my family were happy here, so you don't really ever think about uprooting people.

Everything was in Bradford for me and I knew that one of the big reasons in me signing was that Lee Gilmour was there, who I knew really well from my Bradford days. Then I found out that Fozzard and Baloo, Paul Anderson, travelled too, so they assured me I could go over with them and it was sort of the last box to tick, to ensure I didn't have to move or anything like that. If you speak to people, the first thing they say when you mention you commute to places like St Helens or Hull for work is that they don't know how you do it. But out of my whole rugby career, those six years I had travelling from Bradford to Saints were the happiest time of my life on a professional basis - and 2006 was only the start.

# CHAPTER X

The first year at Saints couldn't have gone much better. We cleaned up, won absolutely everything and pretty much decimated the field around us in Super League. I had a feeling I had a cracking chance of not only being in the Great Britain squad for the tour Down Under for the Tri-Nations that year, but playing in the halves on a regular basis too.

However, I always suspected that in the back of my mind, given how the coach was Nobby - a guy who I worked with at Bradford and who had been hesitant to play me at stand-off - I might find chances hard to come by in the halves in a way. But I had a positive mindset and I said to myself that I'd rather play for Great Britain on the wing or in the centres than be a reserve half-back or something like that, so I looked forward to the tour regardless. I was just really happy to play.

And despite everything we did at Saints in 2006, I didn't even really feel like I was going into the internationals in the best form of my career. Looking back now, I felt like I was in better form a couple of years later for the 2008 World Cup with England. 2008 was the best form I've ever been in. I thought I was okay in 2006, but I knew I hadn't peaked as a player and I still had plenty more to come in the years ahead.

The buzz and vibe on Great Britain and international camps as a whole, I've always found tough to try and explain - but here goes. Because rugby league is a regional game and lots of players end up playing for their hometown team at some point in their careers, everyone is very proud of their area and the part of the world - or the M62 - that they play in.

You end up banging ten bells out of each other at Super League level and the rivalry between Yorkshire and Lancashire teams - and even Wigan v St Helens or Bradford v Leeds, for example - made sure that back when I was playing internationally at least, the feel of the camps could sometimes be very divided. The Saints lads would stick with each other, the Leeds would do the same, as would Wigan and so on and so forth. We didn't mix, or we certainly didn't when I played - and that made it very difficult in my eyes to all click together as good as we could have done.

It wasn't like it was a major problem, but there were definitely barriers in place, without a shadow of a doubt. That's something I experienced throughout my career at international level and whether it hindered us on the field, I couldn't answer that. But it definitely put some barriers up for some people, as I say. I think it's changed these days from speaking to players who play at that level now, but it was hard on occasions. People stuck to their own gangs and stuck to their own teammates and hung around with each other and nobody else.

But obviously there's only one thing this chapter could really be about, as most of that tour from a personal perspective was dominated off the field by a particular comment I made about Bondi Beach, wasn't it!

If you listen to the press and go off the way the media act over there then they can come off quite derogatory towards the English, in my opinion. It's always 'Pommy this, Pommy that', 'you drink warm beer', all the usual crappy gags. I've always found it quite insulting, and I've always thought that they like to stick the boot in quite a bit. So one day I thought sod it, I'll give them a little bit of needle back and see how they react. I didn't realise it would be taken as seriously as what it was and how much they'd get riled up about it!

I did a column for the BBC with a journalist called Dave Woods, where I was asked how the tour was and how I was finding it. Now in all honesty I really was enjoying it, but me being me and wanting to wind someone up, I thought I'd throw something in there to see how they reacted.

I said, 'It's not all it's made out to be. All the Aussies come over to England and say how good it is, but I'd much rather be back in Bradford. I'd rather be on Blackpool Beach than Bondi Beach. They can keep the country to themselves.'

Talk about a serious overreaction from what followed. In all honesty, with it being an interview with an English journalist, I thought it would just go out in England. Turns out it went out all across the world on the BBC website!

I remember a few of the Australian players bit back almost straight away and had a few digs - and I genuinely didn't even see it as a big deal. They give us some shit and rip us up, particularly in the press when we're touring over there as Great Britain or England, so why shouldn't we give them some back! It's all good fun, right!

Anyway, the day after the story had been on the BBC website, I woke up as usual in the morning to get ready for a morning at training and Channel 9 were ringing mine and Lee Gilmour's room at 6am demanding to speak to Great Britain rugby league player Leon Pryce about 'the Bondi story' - shit!

The backstory to me saying it - which I don't think has ever really been said - is that we'd all heard about Bondi when we were back at home in the north of England, so me, Gilly, Jon Wilkin and all the St Helens boys used one of our first days off on tour to head down there and see what the fuss was all about. Now when you see it on TV it looks absolutely sensational does the area. But that's TV, I guess, they glam everything up the best they can.

So we head down there first thing in the morning, all excited, thinking we'll be on this packed-out beach with loads of things to do. But it was ridiculously bare, there was nothing there except loads of flies hovering around in the sticky heat - it wasn't a nice experience! I'm stood there thinking, 'This place Bondi was supposed to be paradise; there's nobody here.' Obviously I know in reality that Bondi is a beautiful place with a beautiful beach, but at the time that we went, it must have been having an off day!

Anyway the morning these reporters were demanding to speak to me I refused obviously, because I knew what it was about. So we went down to training and the amount of TV cameras and reporters there was unbelievable. There were people trying to get interviews with me, my face was plastered all over the back pages of the Aussie papers like the Sydney Morning Herald and the Daily Telegraph. I've never known attention like it. Typically for me, it was all bad press and not good press! Their headlines were saying stuff like, 'GET HIM OUT OF HERE!' and things like that - I felt like a criminal!

Players were saying all sorts of stuff about me - a former Australia player called Mark Geyer said I should fly back home - but only on economy class because I wouldn't know what first class is! It's fair to say they took it poorly.

All the lads were pissing themselves almost immediately and thinking it was great because it took the attention off the team. But obviously from my own perspective, it was me copping it every single day from the Australian public and the press. I would walk down the streets in Sydney and the odd person would be shouting stuff at me. The press were like animals, and it just wasn't very nice at all, and it all came from an innocent joke which seemingly a whole nation took the wrong way. That was leading into the game against the Australians, and they had riled us with all sorts of stuff themselves. I think someone even dubbed us 'amateurs' in the days running up to the game. What a joke.

We had plenty of emotion built up inside of us and with the grief I was getting, I think it galvanised the boys even more - and for me personally it's the number one game of my career. We had to win it, we just had to. There was no other option to keep our tournament alive.

It's the game which has the most single memories and the most standout moments as a whole. There was the big fight at the start between Willie Mason and Stuart Fielden, before Jamie Peacock waded in and levelled Mason off. There was Longy getting flattened by Mason early doors and just watching Longy play the way he did after all that, he was inspirational - it typified him as a player. It was his game. He dominated it and there were some damn good players in the other side, guys like Darren Lockyer. But Longy was incredible, the best player on the field by a mile, even after getting knocked out by big Willie early in the game.

In a sporting sense we hate the Aussies, don't we? I've got great mates who are Australians, but when you pull that England or

Great Britain shirt on, you hate them and you do everything you can to want to beat them. I don't think that will ever change, and I don't think I would want that to change when I'm watching.

The strange thing from a Great Britain perspective that year is that on tour, we had two sets of half-backs who were playing really well. There were the Leeds lads - Danny McGuire and Rob Burrow - and the Saints boys - me and Longy. I think it made sense to play a pair from the same club rather than one of each. But I would say that, because Longy was the best player on tour that year, so I'm campaigning now, over a decade on, to still be his half-back partner for the whole thing!

In the first game against New Zealand, Nobby partnered Danny McGuire with Longy. I was on the wing. They didn't combine as well as teammates would have done, in my opinion, be it me and Longy or McGuire and Burrow. Against Australia in Sydney, Nobby mixed it up and brought me into the halves, which meant we had our full-back - Wello - our half-backs - me and Longy - and our hooker - James Roby - all from the same club. It was a great decision from Nobby because it all just seemed to click.

After that, we played New Zealand in Wellington, but Brian Carney had picked up an injury so we were a winger light. Nobby could have played a couple of other wingers there but decided to go with me, so I ended up back on the wing - and we got smashed. We were awful and by this point I think Longy had decided he'd had enough. It's never easy away from home, I know that, but when Longy pulled us in and just dropped it on us that he was going home one day, we were stunned.

In the heat of the moment we all say things like that. We were having a feedback in Brisbane and he just decided to tell us all unannounced. We responded, winding him up like all the Saints lads used to, just ribbing him saying, 'You won't go' - not expecting that he actually would. In all honesty looking back, we were making a joke about it, but the next day he'd called Nobby, who went up to his room.

Nobby told Longy in 2004 he was one of the best scrum-halves in the world, but hooked him in a game after about 15 minutes and I don't think Sean ever let that settle. I think that might have been something to do with it. He was homesick too, of course he was, but we tried our utmost to try and get him to stay because I thought it was a stupid decision. I think looking back, it was the wrong move.

The night before, Longy had pissed all over his bed in a drunken state and Nobby walked into the room to try and convince him to stay and not make what he thought was a terrible mistake. So here's Nobby, the Great Britain coach, sat on his bed, covered in piss, having this serious chat. Sean was sat on the other bed, which was Jon Wilkin's, while Nobby is laid over these horrible sheets covered in piss! That kind of ended our tour I think there though, when Longy went home.

It's a shame Nobby couldn't talk him round in all seriousness, because I think he might have paired us up again. But we were done for in terms of our chances when he went. He's said that's one of the biggest regrets of his career and in hindsight, our chances went up in smoke at that point. We all tried to convince him to stay, but it stemmed back a little bit further between Nobby and Longy.

I'd just had a full year playing with Longy and we clicked as mates straight away, so personally, it was sad to see a good friend decide to go home because he didn't want to be on the tour anymore, but I respect his decision even now.

But back to the Australia game. Lee Gilmour scored our third try on the night against them which put us 18-12 up - it was a brilliant effort from him - and if you watch the video closely he throws both fists in the air and it looks like he's going to stick his middle fingers up to the crowd, but he thought better of it after all the flak I'd had, so just had his fists up in the air instead! He even told me, 'I was thinking about giving it to them, but I thought better of it!'

Wellington was the penultimate game of that tour, we'd played New Zealand and lost, so we were obviously in a pretty foul mood having practically being eliminated, hanging around waiting for a flight back to Australia to stick around and play a dead-rubber. We weren't allowed to drink and had been put on a drinking ban, but we didn't fancy a long flight to Australia, though. So me, Longy and Gleese decided to spice things up a bit - he will say it was the idea of other people, but it was all him! - by getting a protein shake bottle in the duty-free area of the airport and putting Baileys in it! We said it was chocolate-flavoured protein and amazingly, we got it through. We were sat in the airport talking to Jon Wilkin's mum and dad and we'd already had a couple of sly glasses of red anyway. I got on the plane and remember feeling absolutely knackered - as well as a bit fresh - but after I woke up, I started pumping music into Longy's ears as he was asleep and I was just terrorising people on the plane!

Longy was pretty wild by this point and we started singing really loud. Although Longy insists otherwise, he was singing and shouting on the plane! I decided by that point I wasn't getting involved in any of this crap, so I closed my eyes and had a bit of a snooze on the way back to Australia from New Zealand. By the time I woke up, the plane was getting ready to land and apparently, Martin Gleeson and Longy had caused utter carnage. I think they'd been threatened with ejection from the plane due to all the trouble they had caused.

From thereon out, I was dubbed 'The Firestarter', because they said that I had started causing all the trouble, went to sleep and got those guys in hot water, which is obviously a load of rubbish. I'd used my brain and gone to sleep. I think he pissed some Germans off who were travelling. But on a serious note, his mind had already been made up about coming home, I think.

We ended up in Manly after being eliminated and there were no flights back home straight away. So that night, our season was over and we decided to have a blowout as you would when a long old season on both sides of the world gets done and dusted. However, we got a few bottles of wine delivered to the room and management decided to intervene and stop us from drinking. We just wanted to let our hair down and we couldn't get a flight out of Sydney until Tuesday and this was the Sunday night - so what did people think was going to happen! There's only one answer when there's 30 blokes who've had an 11-month season, isn't there!

It's a very different game now of course, but the drinking culture back then was massively different. We were just a set of clowns having fun. The only way I can compare it is that if a headmaster tells pupils to do something, they will ordinarily do exactly the opposite, won't they! And that's what we did. Management told us not to drink, so what are we going to do?

Drink!

I've got a lot of Australian friends and I've played with a lot of Aussies who are great blokes, and they like to give banter as much as they take it, they're fine with it all. Some of my best friends like Michael Withers and Steve Menzies are Aussies, it was banter.

But that whole dig about Bondi was one for the press to eat up - and they definitely did that. I still get grief about it to this day from some people. I think it's going to go on forever! It's just one of those things. Looking back at it now it was great fun and I don't regret it at all because we were the last team to beat the Australians in Australia. If we'd lost the game, maybe so, but I've no regrets over saying what I did. Who knows, maybe it helped us out to win on that night and create a little piece of history. If it did, I'm glad it helped, because it was a special night.

# CHAPTER XI

Spending so much time travelling between two ends of the M62 can take it out of you, but as I say, these years were among the best of my life, not just my career. That was down to two men in no small part: Lee Gilmour and Nick Fozzard. We were at the forefront of what we dubbed the Yorkshire Bus, which became pretty legendary at St Helens, if I say so myself! But it wasn't just on the road where we had fun - we could cause mayhem pretty much anywhere we went.

I spent a bit of time with Gilly when we were both at Bradford earlier in our careers, but we were both young, so were both loud and opinionated and it wasn't that strong a relationship because we were in at each other so much all the time.

He used to come into training in his Subaru Impreza and he used to act like a real wide-boy, so I'd often nick his car, drive it down onto the speedway track at Odsal and take it for a bit of a spin because it was seriously quick.

When I went to Saints though, we just clicked straight away. He's a really good guy and while he's a pain in the arse and he's never wrong in his own eyes, he's a very good person and someone I would do anything for at the drop of a hat.

I don't think he ever got the credit he deserved as a player either, if I'm being honest. He was very underrated and he was always played in a few different positions and never got the chance to properly shine in one until he went to Saints. From there, he established himself as a top-class second-rower. He had such a distinguished career as a player, winning Super League titles, Challenge Cup titles, a brilliant international career and he was in arguably the greatest St Helens teams in history.

He was very talented and he was a real unsung hero. He ended up being such a dominant, defensive player and he was very detailed in everything he did with his preparation. We roomed together at Saints, with Great Britain and we travelled together all the time, so in reality I ended up spending more time with Gilmour than I did with my wife and kids for a good few years. We were living in each other's pockets. As a result of that we ended up very close. He was an usher at my wedding and he's someone I love to bits.

Fozzard is just a one-of-a-kind bloke. In the early days of travelling across in the Yorkshire bus, the things he used to do were outrageous. He would often try and wind Paul Anderson up - who drove across with us in the early days of the Yorkshire Bus - and mess around in the back of the car to the point where Baloo would have to remind him it was his family car.

One of my first games against Wigan for St Helens was a memorable one because of Foz, too. I always used to shout at him to run hard and assert his dominance on the game, because for everything he did in terms of mucking around, he was some bloody player.

This time though, he'd run down the short side, so I collared him and shouted, 'Foz, run hard you pussy!' - and blimey did he! Incensed by me essentially calling him soft, he runs into Stuart Fielden and knocks him clean out to the point where the doctors were on and he needed gas and air.

He turns around deadpan, slams the ball into my chest and says, 'Is that fucking hard enough for you!' What a bloke. All this time one of the best prop forwards in the world is sparked out on the floor and he was my mate, so I was worried about him, but Foz is shouting at me getting into my ear.

We went to Marbella on a training camp with Great Britain that year in 2006, and Brian Noble was pretty good in that he told us he wanted to go out and have a bit of a bonding night ahead of the games - but obviously not to go too strong with the drink.

Anyway, one of the lads in the squad, Gareth Raynor, was playing really well for Hull FC at that time and was deserving of his call-up. But Gilly mentioned that once they'd all been on a night out in Hull and Gaz wasn't too great with handling his drink at the time. There had been some sort of fall out. So we then met up with the Great Britain lads and, straight away, Gaz apologised and they had a couple of shots to bury the hatchet. But he seriously wasn't a drinker at all, as it turned out.

He was wearing the tightest white jeans and a top that was about three sizes too small for him. Great bloke was Gaz, but his dress sense at that time was out there! Anyway, we had a cracking night and we woke up the next morning in a bit of a sorry state - but it was nothing compared to Gaz.

He and Gilly definitely forgot about that night in Hull, but it turns out that they had a bit of a wild one. As it turned out, I had ended up rooming with Gaz. I tried to wake him up, stirring him from his drunken slumber and screaming at him that we had to be downstairs ready for training - but he barely responded.

I had to go get Richard Horne, who knew him really well, to wake him up because he was dead to the world. He needed a familiar voice and they played together at Hull. Somehow, and I don't know how to this day, Horney managed to get Gaz up and get him sat on the edge of the bed. Then we started to dress the bloke. This is a bloke sprawled on a hotel bed while two other guys put his socks and shirt on for him! He was making all these bizarre noises and things like that, but we managed to get him up, downstairs and ready for training. We knew we had to keep him under a low profile, otherwise Nobby would tear a strip off him!

The walk from the hotel to the training base was about half a mile long, a good 15-minute walk or so - at least if you weren't pissed, that is. As we're walking with the group though, Gaz - who we'd strategically placed at the back of everyone - was getting further and further adrift from the rest of us. By the end of it he was a good 10 minutes behind us. Now Nobby had a tendency that either before or after you go out on the drink, he likes to flog you and get the booze out of you one way or another. That was fine for us, but we knew Gaz - if he ever turned up - wouldn't hack it.

By the time we'd done our warm-up, Gaz had decided this wasn't for him and he couldn't deal with it. He just walked away from the training session, sat down, put a full ice bucket over his head and sat underneath a palm tree for about an hour - while we're all getting flogged in a huge training session! Chris Brooks, the Great Britain doctor, was sat wafting him with a towel thinking he's come down with something while we're all looking on saying, 'The lucky bastard!'

I always remember that trip for another reason too. In the plush hotel in Marbella they had screens on your door saying, 'Good Morning Mr Pryce and Mr Raynor' - or whoever it was you were rooming with. Amazingly, Gilly got paired with Foz to room up. But it was only after Paul Anderson decided he didn't want to play that year, so their room said 'Good Morning Mr Gilmour and Mr Anderson'! We've never let Foz forget that, even to this day - he was picked for Great Britain by default!

At the time he had no idea and he thought he'd been picked on merit - which he should have been anyway because he was playing great - but to walk into your first Great Britain camp and see someone else's name on your room, it was hilarious for us and soul-destroying for him. Foz's ability to laugh at anything thankfully rescued the situation. If it had been someone a bit more sensitive, it could have kicked off with us winding him up as much as we were doing!

Every time us three are together, it's absolute carnage. A couple of years ago we were at Ade Gardner's wedding. We were all in our mid-to-late 30s, so you'd think we'd have calmed down a bit - nope.

We were all sharing a room - and a bed, there were three of us in it! - and we ended up rocking up to bed at about 3:30am after a big night. But then suddenly in the middle of the night - or a bit later at least - we're woken up by the hotel fire alarm. We put the light on and I looked across to Foz and we both said at exactly the same time, 'Where the fuck is Gilly!'

There's a fire alarm going off, Gilly is missing - it doesn't take a genius to work out who's done it! This is the wedding of one of our closest friends and we're getting told to get out of our rooms at 3am. All me and Foz can say to each other, while we're being hurried through the hotel lobby, is that it's definitely Gilly, it has to be. There were children crying in the corridors because they'd been woken up to this deafening racket.

Bear in mind the happy couple are trying to, shall we say, enjoy their night and the whole hotel is stood in the freezing cold in the car park because, as it turned out, Gilly decided he'd boot a fire exit open when he wandered off sleepwalking! Turns out that he'd half come round midway through his sleepwalking tour of the hotel and he got himself flustered, panicked and set the fire alarm off so someone would come and get him! As we looked over the hotel car park, we saw Gilly with no pants, no shirt and no shoes being guided out of a building he'd managed to sleepwalk into by a member of the hotel staff.

Another time we'd been out. For once, I went to bed first - but it wasn't long before I got woken up by the two big idiots. Somehow, Foz had to restrain Gilly as he was using his Yorkshire Bank card to try and open the doors in the hotel instead of his keycard - and he tried every room! So Foz caves in and drags him back to our room, and I took one look at them both after being woken up and just muttered under my breath, 'Fucking pricks'.

We pushed the beds together, Gilly gets in the middle of us and no sooner had we turned all the lights off, Gilly exclaims, 'I think I'm going to be sick lads' - shit! It's pitch black in the middle of the night and I switched a light on and gave Foz the dirtiest look for dragging him back to our room!

Anyway, within seconds Gilly is being sick on a tray we'd ordered for our room service. Fair play, he managed to avoid the carpet on this instance. However, he put the tray on the side and he left it hanging over the edge of the bedside table, and when he decides to throw himself back into bed, he kicks the tray up in the air and it all splats over the floor. Again, what a pair of pricks for dragging all this mess into our room. But it gets worse.

We're all just about drifting off to sleep at last - or at least, me and Foz are. That's until I feel someone - obviously Gilly - climbing over Foz to get out of bed. 'What on Earth could he be doing next,' I'm thinking. It's pitch black and all we can hear is just this tinkling noise on the tray. He's having a piss on the tray he's just been sick on! He then gets back into bed and by this point I'd had enough. I ended up deciding to sleep on the floor!

Travelling together on the M62 - which as anyone knows who's driven on it, is one of the most temperamental, frustrating stretches of motorway in the country - was tough at times: especially when we were trying to get to training on time, or get back to spend time with the family.

If you want a fair indication of how mad we all were when we got together, this story is probably it. It sounds bad saying it, but if there was ever a traffic jam and we were in a rush, we'd fly down the hard shoulder for a mile or two to eat up the traffic with the hazard lights on.

One day we were on the way home and, I've no idea why really, but with the music pumping out loud and everyone getting giddy - it must have been just before a day off - we were doing all sorts of stupid stuff like sticking our head out of the sunroof. But all us lot, we were what you'd call 'Tommy Toppers' - the kind of bloke where if someone said they'd just been to Tenerife, you'd say you've been to Elevenerife! So that quickly turned into standing up out of the sunroof and then I, in all my wisdom, got on top of the roof completely and stuck my face in front of the window. Don't ask me why!

Those idiots in the car then decided to, without any warning, turn the windscreen wipers on and catch me out - and they definitely did. This was while we were going about 40 or 50mph down the hard shoulder, and they were videoing it all the while! It was ridiculous. You'd never know how long the journey would take so you'd just decide to do stupid things to pass the time - although most of the times we were late, Gilly was behind it!

There was a cafe on the M62 we'd go to if we had time before we got to training. Joan's Cafe, it was called. If there was ever one day we didn't go, Gilly would lose the plot; and on this particular occasion, we were a good half-hour behind so we decided to miss the cafe out. Gilly didn't react well, and he flat out refused to miss it. He'd say that we were already late so we may as well be a bit later. 'Don't spoil my preparation', he'd say. That is Lee Gilmour summed up to perfection - he wouldn't budge for anyone.

Before we got together at Saints, we did cross paths at Bradford, but we never really had consistent runs in the team together. It was St Helens where we really clicked, but there were still great moments at Bradford. Like I've touched on, Gilly used to drive a Subaru Impreza - it was the fastest car I've ever driven, and still is - and one day, we decided to take it for a spin while he was late having a shower. Late again, Gilmour, as per usual! We didn't take it for any old spin though. I was doing laps of Odsal around the speedway track as fast as I could, thinking I was some sort of racing car driver. What I didn't realise though is that the track at Odsal - or at least it was way back when we were there - was made up of small pieces of gravel. So when I returned Gilly's car to him after my 'cruise', it was completely chipped to hell. He was furious, but I'm pretty sure he got me back eventually.

The bonds I made during that time at Saints with Foz and Gilly will last me a lifetime, but I can't leave out the other big guy from my time at the club: a certain Sean Long.

I could go on and on about him and what he did for my career. We played with such freedom and I like to inject myself into the game when I feel it's needed. I don't need to stay on one side and Longy could control the game at Saints and I'd follow him around the field. I'm not a dominant, rigid six - I'm a roaming stand-off and that just didn't happen when I played at Hull later in my career.

I played with some massive players at Saints too, which obviously helped me. But the number one player I played with was Longy - and not just at Saints, in my entire career. To be honest, if I hadn't played with Longy for the first couple of years of my career at St Helens then I don't think I would have had the career I had after that.

When I used to play against him or watch him on TV earlier in my career, I used to think he was a bit of an arsehole, if I'm being perfectly honest! He was a show-off, wasn't he? The guy with stupid hair. I mean a white guy running around with dreadlocks - come on! He changed his hair all the time as well.

But that perception of him was from the outside looking in - which is how fans see him, because they don't know that he's anything but that. I got to know him really well when I joined St Helens and I realised he is a really good person. I try to only surround myself with good people in life and while Sean plays with this image of not giving a damn what other people think and how other people perceive him, deep down below the surface he is a very loyal, honest person - and he's a good bloke who really does care about those who matter to him. He can be crazy, but everyone is crazy on some level, aren't they!

Rugby league players are out there as a bunch anyway and Longy pretends he doesn't care - but he does care. I just want to get across how much respect I've got for him because it goes without saying that he helped me in my career, without a shadow of a doubt. I wouldn't have wanted to shoehorn these tributes about him into a random chapter - he goes right in alongside Gilly and Foz as part of the reason why Saints was so bloody good.

There's some little stories about him which are just hilarious too. On the 2006 Tri-Nations tour when we were with Great Britain - the Blackpool-Bondi one - all the St Helens lads decided to go for a walk on the beach on a day off. There were guys like me, Jon Wilkin, James Roby and Longy. Suddenly, we heard this guy shout, 'Sausage! Sausage', and we had no idea who it was - but Longy knew. Who the hell shouts 'Sausage!' at someone for no reason on a beach in Sydney?

Well, turns out it was Longy's dad, who he hadn't seen for something like two years and he just randomly turned up on a beach in Sydney - despite not living there - at the same time as his son. He's called Sean Bernard Long and his brother is called Karl Bernard Long, and his dad is called Bernard! What a family. If you read his book he sounds crazy but there's no player I've got more respect for than Longy and I love him to bits.

The rugby brain that guy had was absolutely incredible - he was a genius. He saw things that other people couldn't - and I'd consider myself to be someone who knew the finer details of the game quite well. He could coach the coaches and could tell people how to play. Daniel Anderson came in and practically the first thing he said to people was that he wasn't going to bother with the attacking side of things, because 'Longy can take care of all that' - I've never known that ever happen before. He'd just sort the defence out would Daniel - and that didn't work out too badly, did it!

I don't see the problems Longy had off the field as problems. People might see it as that, but they're just part of his personality. Not everyone in rugby league is meant to be a model professional, surely.

Certain people dedicate themselves to the game and nothing else, which is fine, but if we were all the same person, life would be pretty boring, wouldn't it. He's perceived as really crazy, but there's a lot more depth to him than what people think. He's one of my best mates, but deep down he's a very good, loyal man. Some of the crazy stuff he's done gets spoken about before his actual strengths as a person - as a rugby player he was a genius and as a person he's a very, very good bloke, despite all the crazy haircuts and the wild antics he got up to.

If he hadn't done half the stuff he did off the field, he might not have been the player he was. He was a character, a maverick, but sometimes geniuses have a side to them that makes them a little bit crazy. I'm crazy, but I definitely wouldn't say I was a genius though!

# Lee Gilmour

## (Bradford, St Helens and Great Britain teammate)

I've got one best mate in rugby without a shadow of a doubt - and it's Leon Pryce.

I first met him at Bradford all those years ago when he was the new kid on the block, and I'd seen him come through the ranks while I was playing at Wigan. He won the Young Player of the Year award and played international rugby from such a young age, so it was obvious as to how talented he was.

When I got to Bradford, I suppose it can be a bit intimidating if you're walking into a new club as big as Bradford were, but he was someone I clicked with straight away and as a local lad, he made me feel really, really welcome.

I'll never forget the tale that I'm sure he's told his side of - in relation to my Subaru Impreza! One day after training, I'm having a bit of food and playing some cards, but I couldn't find my car keys anywhere. I go outside to have a look and see if I've dropped them and when I have a look down onto the pitch, I hear this noise - it's Leon whirling around the speedway track in my Subaru.

What I'll never forget is that after he'd been driving around and chipping my car to bits, he just walked back over, nice and blasé, passed me my car keys and walked away as if it was a normal thing to do - to nick someone's car.

It was how chilled he was about it which I'll never forget. I didn't even get a chance to give him a spray because he'd already shot off into the distance - cheeky bastard! I suppose that was one of the first instances of him being 'The Firestarter' as he was christened at St Helens!

As a player, I've been sharing some old clips in WhatsApp groups. Leon does too, and there's nothing he likes more than finding old footage of himself and reminding everyone what a great player he is.

I spent three years with him at Bradford and four at St Helens and it's easy to skirt over just how good he was. Not many players can be that good in so many different positions. Some players can be a utility of course, but to play the amount of different positions he did at the level he did was remarkable. He mastered wing, full-back and stand-off. He was such a dangerous runner and overall he was just a massive game-breaker on the field. When he got to play with Longy, that partnership was perfect, because Sean could marshal the game and all Leon had to do was come in and out when the time was right and he'd turn the game.

I think another reason we got on so well was because we followed similar career paths. We were both at Bradford and we'd both played internationals, but we were in and out of the team, playing in different positions all the time. We might need to move positions due to injuries, but this was more than that. I went at the end of 2003 and a couple more years passed and Leon got to the point where he was at an age he needed regular game-time in one position.

Ian Millward was the coach before Leon actually joined, and he actually spoke to me about signing Leon. I was still good friends with him after our time at Bradford, so I was obviously going to give him a glowing reference, wasn't I!

I spoke to Leon too and sounded him out about the move. We were a good side before we moved with Jason Hooper predominantly playing stand-off, but he was a rough and tough half-back whereas Leon, as I say, had that game-breaking ability about him which was crucial for us.

He's my best friend within the game, but he's also one of my closest friends, full stop. We're very like-minded and I think that's why we get on so well. Carly, his wife, used to refer to me as his other half because we spent so much time in each other's pockets, travelling along the M62 all the time. But he's a great bloke. He's The Firestarter and he always will be. If there was a bit of mischief to be had at Saints, you could bet any money Leon would be right in the thick of it.

Suddenly, when it all exploded, off he was into the night without managing to take any of the rap for it!

I honestly don't think there's anyone else quite like Leon Pryce in the Super League era. There hasn't been a stand-off who could do the things he could do. He's unique in that he's got a massive stature, he's 100 kilos with these extraordinary long limbs and you match that up with someone who has incredible skill: it's a rare mix.

To play international standard in so many positions, in some respects, that ensures he stands on his own. I don't think there will be anyone else quite like him. He's one of the best stand-offs I've seen.

# CHAPTER XII

At the start of the 2008 season, I recall we went off to Wales for a camp. When the club said we were going away for a camp we thought it would be sun-kissed weather somewhere nice and hot, because in all honesty it's never absolutely brilliant weather-wise in the United Kingdom, is it! The previous year we'd been taken to Dubai, so we're dreaming of something like that again, but it absolutely pissed it down all the way through!

Unfortunately for the powers that be, it just wasn't in our DNA to let the hours pass by and stay in. They said don't leave the premises - but we did. They said be back at midnight - but it was later. They said don't get pissed - but we did. One night they told us to be back in bed for midnight no matter what - you know what happened next.

We had all the intention of following orders and having a nice quiet night, but we ended up getting ourselves off into Cardiff and getting absolutely trollied. We were in walkabout smashing drinks back. After all this drinking we end up staggering back to a taxi - or at least I do! I'm sat in the taxi waiting for those two idiots and as they staggered back out, they decide to wander back into the club. I promise I tried to stop them, but they were too influential! Off we went back in, and we kept drinking for hours and we rocked up at, well, I don't know! At one point I remember one of us declaring that we were the Yorkshire Bus, and we didn't go home when we were told!

The next morning at breakfast, in comes Daniel Anderson, marching towards us three and he shouts, 'You, you and you! Get your arses into the corridor, now!' We know what's coming.

He starts asking what time we came in and Foz holds his hands up and says it was about 1am - it was a lot later than that in actual fact! - and apologises for breaking the curfew. We're then sat back down at the table trying to work out who's ratted us out and told the coach, so we all confronted the lads - Yorkshire Bus against the world was the mentality by this point - and asked them who did it.

'Don't you know?' one of them said. What the hell were they on about? They said we came back in the middle of the night and started knocking on everyone's door in the hotel - and I mean everyone's - shouting 'Yorkshire, Yorkshire, Yorkshire!' To be fair, I think Gilly snuck off to bed, but before that he kept falling out of the taxi and wandering off. There must have been about 20 red lights according to Foz on the way back to the hotel, and Gilly in his pissed-up state thought every time we stopped, it was time to get out because we were there. It must have happened about 15 times - it was hilarious.

Once, we were away in France to play Catalans Dragons, and we were told to not be drinking or anything like that. We had been on a walk around the town and we had sleeping tablets that we used to get from the doctor if we needed them, but he said that people had been misusing them. He used to give you one, watch you take it after a game so he knew you'd taken it.

Anyway, on this instance we got some sleeping tablets and someone had made these blue ones up where if you touched them, they left what was essentially a blue dye on your hands for about 48 hours - like a residue.

You had blue lips too, and people were coming into training and we were asking people to show us their fingers and lips to check if they'd been on them. On this instance there were four or five players - I wouldn't want to name them - who refused to drink and they were playing cards, but they'd crushed up a load of these tablets and put them in a big bottle of water - and they were doing shots from a bottle of water. We came back and I remember Nick Fozzard saying to these four, sensible blokes, 'What the fuck are you doing!'

We'd taken one so we slept fairly easily, but they were completely knocked to bits by them. In the first half of the game against Catalans I remember watching some of the lads and it was like watching them in slow motion. I remember someone threw a pass to Foz and instead of a bullet pass it was floating through the air! When we watched it on video the week after, Jesus it was unbelievable. Incredibly though, Daniel Anderson didn't know we'd done all this and he was lambasting us on video saying, 'What the fuck is going on here', and things like that. Anyway, as he's tearing into us he comes out with what he thought was an innocent line, but it cracked us up: 'You all look like you're fucking half asleep out there!' We all looked at each other and thought, if only he knew! Amazingly we won the game. That was a complete one-off though, I've got to stress that.

I just think my time at Saints was so good because although I'd been at Bradford throughout the glory years and won everything there was to win with the Bulls, when I moved to St Helens at the end of 2005 things just seemed to happen on a whole other level.

But the style of rugby at St Helens was completely different to anything I'd ever experienced too at that time. The way the players played and the way the players like Sean Long, Paul

Sculthorpe, Keiron Cunningham and Paul Wellens talked about the rugby they played and how great a club it was made it a really attractive club to be a part of.

You're on Sky Sports almost every week and you're playing with some incredible players - literally once-in-a-generation players like Longy. It was a great time to be at that club and you start to believe in yourself a bit more. By the end of the 2006 season we'd won every trophy available and we followed that up with the World Club Challenge at the start of 2007 by beating Brisbane at Bolton, which really underlined how good we were then in my opinion. I felt really good going into that 2007 season. I felt I played fairly decent in my first year there, but I don't think I was really as pivotal a part of the team as I wanted to be.

Don't fall into the trap of thinking that Brisbane were just another NRL side over here for a pre-season warm-up game, either. They sent all the big boys, all the big guns - and we beat them. Champions of the world, get in!

And after that first year of bedding in - when we won the lot - I really felt like I began to properly hit the best form of my career. I was about three or four kilos overweight in that first season at Saints, at least compared to what you need to be weight-wise as a stand-off at the top end of Super League. I had a cracking off-season though and I lost all that weight and that's where I felt like I began to be really effective in a Saints shirt.

In 2008, things went to another level again. I was named Player of the Year at St Helens, which at that time, was an award not to be sniffed at. I'm still really proud looking back that I won that, but I was also in contention for the Man of Steel award too.

I'd trained really hard in pre-season and crucially, I had two knees which both worked and held out all year.

What I really want to make clear though is that despite being a Bradford lad and a Bradford fan, I feel like St Helens is just as much 'my' club, if that makes sense. That's where I've had the best years of my life and played the best rugby of my career. When we went out on that field it was like an accumulation of everything that is good in rugby league happening all at once.

Nine times out of ten it clicked and it just worked how we wanted it to, and how we practised it in training. To be able to go out and just play without being restricted to playing on particular sides was a joy. We were successful, it was fun going to training - even with all the commuting - we had a great coach in Daniel Anderson, the banter was incredible and that made us even tighter.

As I say, those few years at St Helens are the best of my career because everything came together and created a club and a vibe which, at times, was pretty much near-unstoppable.

Daniel was a massive part of the success the club had too. Before him there were other great Australian coaches at the club like Shaun McRae and Ian Millward, and although I never got to play under those guys I just sensed that Daniel brought a different feel to the club and helped set the whole place up for that golden period of success. He didn't over-coach people and it can't have been easy to coach a team of superstars like Longy, Wello and Scully.

It's about managing egos and managing expectations. Good players naturally have a bit of an ego about them, and Daniel knew how to control everyone all at once. I could be difficult to handle, Longy could be the same and guys like Keiron Cunningham and Jamie Lyon had a presence about them too. They were big characters. All those guys in one room can go one of two ways: it can be the recipe for sustained success or it could be disastrous. To get the best out of all those people at the same time is not easy, and that's where Daniel deserves a mountain of credit in my eyes.

He played it straight down the line with me. If I was playing crap, he would tell me - something I thought he enjoyed telling me! - but if I was playing well he knew the time was right to praise me and the way I was going. At Bradford we had this up-and-out sliding defence system which worked well. Daniel brought a defensive structure with him to St Helens from the NRL which I'd never really seen before.

You used your inside and outside shoulder and you defended in spaces, not just picking one man and sticking with him. It was revolutionary in a lot of ways - a lot of the boys had never seen anything like it. Whichever part of the field you were on, each defender had a particular amount of space. I won't spend too much time talking about tactics in this book as I always found training and stuff a bit tedious, but I had to mention this because it changed the way so many top players at St Helens viewed defending.

Some of those guys have gone on and had coaching careers elsewhere too and I'd be surprised if they haven't introduced it to their teams because it was that good. If I ever get into coaching I would definitely incorporate Daniel's methods.

Once I learned to play that way, it was obvious that the system was around four or five years ahead of its time as a whole compared to the rest of Super League. The best thing I liked about Daniel though was that for the first time in my career, someone would come down on me really hard which I needed. The fact he was a revolutionary coach compared to the rest was a huge bonus too, clearly.

Those three years - 2006, 2007 and 2008 - were probably the best three consecutive years in the club's history in my eyes. I mean we won it all in 2006, nobody could come close to us with the team that we had. That 2006 team is the best single team that has played in Super League in my opinion - how can anything touch it? You've got some supreme talent, a team where practically every single player is or has been an international. It was incredible. People look back even now with such high regard for that Saints team and it was a pleasure to play in and an even greater privilege to be a part of.

There's probably three teams people think of as the best, and they all won a treble: Bradford in 2003, Saints in 2006 and Leeds in 2015. To some they're hard to split, but if you go through the stats that season they're just incredible. We lost four games all season in all competitions. One was by a point to Hull FC, one was by two points to Bradford, one was by three points to Huddersfield and one was by four points against Catalans - but that was the week before the Challenge Cup Final at Wembley.

Nobody beat us by more than a handful of points all year. We were on it every single week. Who's ever done that? Who will do that again? We followed it up shortly after by beating a full-strength Brisbane Broncos team with Darren Lockyer, Karmichael Hunt, Sam Thaiday - the lot. They wanted that trophy, but they couldn't get it from us. We were world champions fair and square that season.

When I was out in Bradford when I played for the Bulls I obviously got noticed and people asked for my autograph and things like that, but in St Helens it was on a whole other level. It's a rugby league town through and through and we were treated like professional footballers - even more so when we were playing well. Because everything was going so good and there was such a buzz around the whole town because of it, it was literally like being a Premier League footballer, that's the only way I could describe it.

I remember the night after we won the 2008 Challenge Cup and we went out on the Sunday night in St Helens, and oh my God, it was incredible. We were treated like superstars everywhere we went - we felt like we were in a band - it was insane! The thing is with me is that if I feel loved by fans or people give you affection and love when you're playing rugby, that helps to bring out the best in me as a player, I think. The Saints fans have always been great with me and they've been nothing but nice to me, singing songs about me and being really great everywhere I went around the town. I'll never forget that as long as I live.

I respond to that as a player and before I got to Saints, I wasn't really used to it, which I understood. I'd played a bit of here, there and everywhere at Bradford, so it was understandable, but playing regularly at St Helens, they just loved me from the start. I wasn't expecting it really because I'd have expected them to be more into their hometown boys like James Roby and James Graham, but the love they showed me, I felt like I was from St Helens at times, to be honest.

Whenever I go back there now I still feel like I'm a massive part of that club. It's where I've had the most enjoyment playing and played the best rugby, as well as winning trophies where I feel like I've actually contributed as a pivotal player in a side. The only thing that makes me feel a little bit sad is while I'm sure the fans can still feel the history of the club and achievements we had, they've changed stadiums now and moved on from Knowsley Road. That ground had such a unique feel to it and it had such an intimidating aura about it that some teams couldn't really handle.

The older grounds do need updating, but when you upgrade or move on you lose something you can't quite put a finger on. It's like a closeness and a bond between fans and players because of all the history and the fact the crowd are right on top of you. It lingered around at Knowsley Road and on the big nights, you could feel it giving you a lift. People always sit and talk about cliches like that as bollocks, but I'd say those people have never experienced a big night at Knowsley Road. It was a special place.

I remember playing Leeds and Bradford there not long after I joined and the buzz the place gave me was something else when it was packed. It was an amazing ground. I got man of the match against Leeds and going into the Bradford game, I didn't really know how to feel.

This was my first game playing against the Bulls in my entire life and the emotions I experienced going into that game were pretty significant, because well, it was just weird. But in the game I remember scoring a try and naturally, you wonder what you're going to do in regards to celebrating or not!

Luckily all the lads jumped on me in time before I could make a decision, but I wouldn't have done anyway. There's got to be an element of respect. It just felt like a bittersweet moment given how I'd done something good for my new club but I wanted to show a bit of respect to Bradford fans for the support they'd given me throughout my career.

# CHAPTER XIII

I was this cocky little shite out on the field for most of my career and was oblivious to most of the stuff going on around me, but there was one incident I really remember which changed my mentality about being conscious of things that were happening to me, and that was in 2007.

I'd only left Bradford a couple of years since and the reactions I got when I played against them weren't fantastic to say the least. But when I grabbed Sam Burgess in the bollocks, that's when I copped it. I was embarrassed more than anything. It was on the BBC with half the world watching on in a big Challenge Cup game, and I got a four-match ban and a £500 fine.

'What the hell am I doing here,' I remember saying to myself one night. I don't need to be missing games or paying out money and I've never been banned since then, not once. Daniel Anderson tore me a bit of a new one too. I used to do stupid stuff when I was playing, as I've touched on already - and this was the last one really. I've never been banned since, so that proves I learned my lesson. My last disciplinary was in 2007, and I'm still playing now and haven't had a disciplinary since, so that proves it, I think.

The other big one before was when I took Jamie Lyon's head off when I was playing for Bradford and got sent off. I nearly knocked his noggin into another atmosphere, and I got sent off elbowing Danny Orr whilst again playing for Bradford against Castleford. I was sometimes too intense - crazy even - and I used to think it would earn me respect, but it really doesn't. But I was a kid throughout most of these instances, it was who I was at that point in my life.

I thought playing that way was getting me over people, but it just made me look fucking stupid. Age has changed me, 100 per cent. If I looked back at the 18-year-old Leon now who did all this stuff, I wish I could go back and tell him a few home truths. There were a lot of lessons I needed to learn to get to this point in my life.

I like that younger version of me in many ways as he was so fearless and so blind to everything that was about to come his way, but there was certainly some stuff I know now that I wish I could have done back then.

Before I got in trouble, I was confident and cocky, but there were a lot of lessons I needed to learn to get to the point I'm at now. We all make mistakes, but it's part of who you are and who you become, I guess.

I don't think you really learn until you make mistakes in life - I'm not saying you should - but if you do make mistakes and pay for them, it makes you a better person, even if it's cost me a lot of money and a lot of stress along the way. I would never recommend making the mistakes I've made to anyone because I don't want my kids looking on the Internet and seeing that their old man has been in all sorts of trouble off the field, but you obviously never think of that when you're a teenager, oblivious to everything around you and how everything has a consequence in life. It's part of who I am.

I don't have a lot of regrets in my career, but when I started playing as a teenager I was a very grubby player in the way I played. I was getting done for offences like these and it's something I'm really not proud of.

If my kids go on YouTube and want to watch clips of me playing rugby, what they'll see are the bad things like the things where I've been sent off or done stupid things like grabbing Sam Burgess' balls. When I took Jamie's head off I just knew I had to watch him closely because he was the Man of Steel and I didn't want to be embarrassed and I ended up knocking his head off the first chance I got. It was just stupid and if there's one piece of advice I'll give to my children, it's not to do those things.

I did the same to Kevin Sinfield one year when we played at Valley Parade against Leeds. I took him out blatantly late and off the ball, and I hit him high and I always carried that with me. The last time I played against Kevin while he was a Leeds player and I was playing for Hull FC - I knew he was leaving rugby league at the end of 2015 - I pulled him to the side and apologised for what I did in that game 15 years earlier because it was a shitty, stupid thing to do.

Kevin being the guy he is, he told me not to worry about it, but I carried it with me because it was childish, wasn't it? That's not the way to play the game in my opinion - I would advise all young players to play the game properly and don't risk getting a reputation for doing the bad things, because they easily overshadow all the good you can do.

The incident with Sam Burgess was the same. I knew I was going to cop it, but I knew I had to do something to put him off his game. It was a big game. It was the semi-finals of the Challenge Cup and there was a lot of build-up and hype and I was playing against my hometown club. Sam was the new kid on the block taking the league by storm and I just wanted to put him off. It wasn't to hurt him or injure him, but in my mind, because he was so inexperienced, I knew something like that would unsettle him. But looking back, it was obviously something I'm not proud of.

In my head, I don't know what I was thinking at the time. I knew I didn't want to hurt him, so it was the only thing I could think of to put him off. I got a call from Daniel Anderson shortly after the game telling me that I'd been caught doing it live on the BBC. Stupid me didn't realise the game was on TV in the heat of the moment - and I was up in front of the disciplinary panel.

I got a four-game ban for that and he ripped into me. 'Don't you ever do anything like that ever fucking again' - and boy I listened to Daniel, because well, he was the boss. But I swore to myself that I wouldn't do something as stupid as that again in my career and I stuck to it. Looking back, I think it cost me in quite a big way. That's because 2008 was my best season as a player. I'd done everything right going into the season and I'd prepared well and it was showing with the way I played that year in the St Helens team.

I was on for the stand-off shirt for England in the World Cup and, with no disrespect to James Graham, who is a great friend of mine still to this day, I thought I could have just edged him for the Man of Steel award that season. I knew I was up there with the way I was playing and I had a fair chance of grabbing it.

But when you're getting voted by your peers for an award, if you're seen to be doing things like that - dirty, unsportsmanlike play - people become less fond of you. It's one of my regrets really, because it was that year when I got in trouble off the field leading up to the decision for Man of Steel, and it's pretty obvious that it didn't do me any favours either.

It doesn't look good when I'm in the national newspapers up on an assault charge - I'll go into that later - and I'm trying to win an award voted for by my fellow professionals. That's clearly going to have an impact on my chances.

I will always remember that night as clear as day. I was eventually nominated alongside both Jammer and Jamie Peacock at Leeds, which was pretty decent company to be in. But at the awards ceremony itself, when my name was read out as one of the nominees for the award, there was a table which actually booed me. Even though it sounds funny as an individual when you're up for honours, it's actually soul-destroying and it's something that still lives with me to this day.

It's a proud moment, one of the proudest of my career, to be recognised as one of the best players in Super League. But when I heard that smattering of boos from people, I knew that, given how it was an award voted for by people who were in the room at that time, I had no chance of winning it.

My dad was with me that night too, and it wasn't really great to hear my name being booed when my own parents were in attendance. That was one thing that I would have loved to have got my hands on throughout my career - I'm not saying that I deserved it that year or I didn't, but I just wonder what if sometimes. I gave myself a great chance because I trained really hard and played well, but maybe it was never going to be enough.

But going into the World Cup that year, I had the best feeling I'd ever had that not only did we stand a decent chance at the World Cup, but I'd be a big part of the team. That year, Tony

Smith had given me the stand-off shirt midway through the season after I got in front of Danny McGuire, which was no mean feat because he was playing really well himself.

I was in the best form of my career and I was so confident for both myself and the team, but it remains one of the biggest disappointments of my entire career.

When push came to shove, it was a massive let-down and essentially, it was a big failure. On a personal level I played nowhere near how I could have done and how I had for Saints that season. We got hammered by Australia in Melbourne and eventually got knocked out by New Zealand and it just wasn't a fun tour whatsoever.

A tour is not just about rugby, it's about seeing different places and exploring different cultures together as a group and a team, but there was so little of that from my personal experience and the camp was quite divided. Rugby comes first obviously, but you've got to have a good culture, and without using the word too lightly, it was a pretty depressing experience all the way throughout. It's not one I'll remember with too many fond memories.

My performances in comparison to my Super League form were massively disappointing too. I felt like I didn't represent myself well on the biggest stage in the year I peaked.

Plus, I got injured and missed out after the first two games, which made things even worse. I think I would have been dropped anyway, to be honest, because I had a stinker early doors, but I picked up a bad rib which ruled me out of the game against New Zealand in Newcastle.

When I played at St Helens and the way I played, being behind a dominant, controlling scrum-half like Sean Long, it really suited me. Unfortunately, I spent that tour playing in the halves with Rob Burrow, who is a great player without a shadow of a doubt, but I just think we were too similar as a pairing. He was a great player, but Longy was a creative, controlling half-back, which brought out the best in me - and the fact we had played together at club level every week obviously helped me when I was playing with him.

I probably had it in the back of my mind it would be my last World Cup, because I was getting near to 30 and World Cups don't come around too often, do they? Although in all fairness, by the time I got home from Australia that year I wasn't really that bothered if I would have never played in a World Cup again, if the atmospheres and the moods were going to be like that. As things turned out, it was the last time I ever played representative rugby league for my country. It was a shame to see things end like that really.

I always thought that, given how well I was playing around that time in 2007 and 2008, that I could have played rugby union quite easily in that period. I felt like I was capable of making the transition. I play the kind of position that could have transferred to the other code quite easily. My contract was coming to an end at the end of 2008 and I was looking at my options to see what suited me best. I'd had a cracking year for St Helens in 2007 and while there was tentative interest from union, thankfully it all got sorted really quickly and I got tied down with Eamonn and St Helens.

In my experience of playing the game, there are two different types of chairman. I never really saw Chris Caisley at Bradford, and I'm not saying there's anything wrong with that, but Eamonn was exactly the opposite. After every game, Eamonn was stood by the side of the field shaking hands with the players and I had quite a lot of dealings with him.

He's the kind of guy that got business done properly and he'd always be there. I liked that - although again, that's not me saying Chris Caisley didn't do business properly. Eamonn got the right squads, the right players and he got whoever he wanted to get in. I've got a lot of respect for the way Eamonn handles his business at that club. He made sure that deal got sorted out. I went into the meeting hoping for a new two-year deal and Eamonn, without any fuss, threw a four-year contract down for me. I nearly fell off my seat with surprise! I told Eamonn that I would be moving on if they couldn't agree to my terms and what I was hoping to get to stay with the club - I always wanted to stay really - and it felt like they were walking over broken glass to keep me.

That was to do with Eamonn. I think he's a great businessman and he's done wonders for St Helens - both the club and the town. I don't know where they'd be without Eamonn. He's a massive part of why they're always at the top of the table and he'd always make sure the players felt loved. He always treated me very well and a lot of the success, even though we had a good squad, was down to Eamonn and he really deserves some proper credit.

While there are two types of chairmen, in my experience there are also two types of club. Bradford were a real family club with everyone off the field and stuff like that, but St Helens were all about business. Don't get me wrong, they were both equally professional, but Bradford felt more of a family club, where we were all involved - wives, children and friends - and Saints felt more of a rugby club where it was about getting performances and winning trophies.

At Saints we were all tuned in exactly the same way. We'd get onto that field - whether it was in a game or in training - and there'd be me, Wello, Longy, Wilko, Jammer, and so many more and we'd be screaming at each other. I think that really suited me as a player, because it kept me on my toes.

We'd rip strips off each other at training and in a game. I imagine the opposition would hear us swearing and shouting at each other and they'd think we all hated each other! But that's the way we were programmed there. It was win at all costs and I absolutely loved how it brought the best out of me at that time in my career. Everyone at that club - from the kit-man to the board members to the players - just wanted to win however they could and anything less wasn't acceptable. The mood on a Monday morning in training if we'd lost was absolutely awful - it was like our season had ended sometimes.

I saw rumours emanating in the press towards the end of my second year at Saints that I'd asked for an early release from my contract. What a load of bollocks. There was concrete interest from rugby union though, because Worcester came to the table with a two-year deal to go and play for them, which was pretty big at the time.

It was pretty big money and it was when Clive Griffiths - who had played rugby league for St Helens himself way back, so obviously knew a fair bit about me - was at the club as their head of rugby, and the offer was serious and it was a really, really good wage, I can say that much: obviously without revealing exact figures. Worcester weren't the only club either. I spoke to Shaun Edwards when he was at Wasps about going down to London and playing for them too. I could have gone there easily. It just didn't feel right though.

Around 2007, loads of rugby league players were making the switch to union. Chris Ashton was the big one having left Wigan really on top of his game and union as a sport were obviously actively targeting rugby league players more and more. I actually met with the England coach, Andy Robinson, as well and the national team were really keen for me to come across and it was a serious option. However, the problem from my perspective was that I'd not achieved everything I'd wanted to in the sport back then. It was the end of the 2007 season, my second at Saints, when this was all happening. I'd wanted to win the Lance Todd Trophy, play for Great Britain in a decent role and on a consistent basis and there were things in my brain that I'd not ticked off the list I'd set out for myself from a young age. Luckily as it worked out, my best years were to come at St Helens and I didn't really want to go.

Financially there was the potential if I'd made it to the England team to earn a lot of money, because you can get tens of thousands of pounds for every single cap you get playing for the England rugby union team, which is pretty serious money in comparison to rugby league, clearly. But that wasn't my goal, to earn loads of money. My goal was to win trophies and be the best player I could be in league.

Our Karl obviously ended up going to Gloucester shortly after all this was happening with me, but there were things in rugby league I wouldn't have left the sport without doing.

The other option for British rugby league players is the NRL, but I can honestly say that hand on heart, I never really considered making the move to Australia. That might surprise a few people and it might make me one of only a handful of people to think like that, but it wasn't on my radar. I had never watched Australian rugby league and I'd never given any thought to going there. In all honesty, rugby union was probably marginally more interesting to me, because I just didn't want to leave this country with a young family and being a bit of a home bird – no clubs ever came calling or anything.

It was an awesome feeling to be given the length of contract they did, and while money-wise I can look back and think what would have happened if I'd gone to rugby union, deep down in my heart, I know that staying with Saints was 100 per cent the right decision. It brought the best out of me as a rugby league player and truly helped me achieve my potential in the sport. Money's not everything. I've had the career I dreamed of - maybe I'd have liked to have won a couple more Grand Finals that I ultimately lost against Leeds! - but I couldn't have asked to have done more.

# Sean Long

## (St Helens and Great Britain teammate)

I'm obviously a little bit older than Leon, so when I was playing representative rugby for Great Britain and England, I was always hearing stories about this kid at Bradford who was in their under-19s and was absolutely killing it.

People were telling me what a special talent this Leon Pryce kid was, but I didn't have a clue who he was in all honesty. I just knew he was this tall, sprightly kid from Bradford who was absolutely destroying the competition he was playing in at that time. Watching him, it became obvious he had such confidence in himself and such a swagger for a young kid - I knew pretty early on from watching him that he was special.

As I watched him develop at Bradford, it became pretty obvious that while they couldn't find a position for him to play each and every week, they just had to get him in the team somehow because he was so good. I think in the Grand Finals he played in against Saints, he was on the centre or even on the wing - but he was always one of the big threats we had to keep an eye on when we played them.

Lo and behold, at the end of 2005, we actually ended up signing this kid and even then, we at Saints didn't know what position he was going to be playing in. But Daniel Anderson had teed him up to play in the halves with me as I'd heard Leon fancied a stab at stand-off, and that was the main pull to get him into the club I think. Whether he was naturally a half-back I don't know, but he fit in perfectly to our system. I played predominantly with the ball in hand, Keiron Cunningham helped out at hooker and we effectively played with two full-backs: Leon and Paul Wellens. Leon would just drop into the line at the right moment and be devastating.

The impact he had at that club was there for all to see in my opinion. We loved a laugh and a joke around Leon, but when it was time to train hard, boy did we all switch on. We'd have a good laugh and Leon liked that, but when he knew it was time to go to work, he certainly did. We were crying out for a running half-back like Leon when he came in at the start of 2006 and as a result of it, we were genuinely untouchable that year - and that's no word of a lie.

I've looked through footage of the season since then and the games we played in, we were just incredible. We had that many threats. If they stopped me, they couldn't stop Leon. If they stopped Leon, they couldn't stop Wello - it just went on and on. The outside backs were incredible, the pack did their job. It was just a team where everyone complemented one another.

We didn't try to outdo each other, we just gave the ball to whoever was in the most space - and Leon could recognise that. It's why I think he's one of the two best halves I ever played with, the other being Tommy Martyn - and I played with some bloody good half-backs, so to be in the top two is big!

He was always there more often than not. He'd come off that big left foot of his and go straight through and come up with the big plays in the big games. In the Grand Finals and the cup finals, Leon came alive. The one against Hull in 2006, where the game was in the balance and he produced the show-and-go and went the length of the field, was a great example. We knew then we'd got that game won and Leon turned it.

But always from the field, Leon was part of why we had such a good laugh. The culture we had at Saints was that we'd train hard during the day, but we'd be more than capable of having a couple of beers and enjoying ourselves on the night, and Leon bought into it really well. We became really good friends almost straight away and he's still someone I'd class in that bracket now. He obviously had the Yorkshire Bus in Lee Gilmour, Paul Anderson and Nick Fozzard behind him, but he was a breath of fresh air on and off the field when he came into Saints.

He was brilliant. He'd always come and stop over in St Helens - although he wasn't a massive boozer, he just liked going out and being part of the team culture we'd built up at the club. St Helens is a club like no other. I've left and come back and everyone is mates on and off the field there - and like I say, Leon just fitted into it really well. We loved taking the piss out of people and we were quite ruthless on the field; if someone didn't do the job we needed them to do, me and Leon as half-backs would get up them like you wouldn't believe.

He was someone who wanted to get the best out of himself, but also out of everyone around him - and me, Keiron, Leon and Wello would often dish out the verbals if we didn't think people were pulling their weight. All this talk about leadership groups is common within the game now, but in reality, we were doing it a whole decade earlier during the years under Daniel Anderson. Leon was a big part of that.

I'd put him in the top five players in Super League history - how couldn't you? He's won absolutely everything there is to win: Harry Sunderland Trophy, Lance Todd Trophy, Challenge Cups, Grand Finals, World Club Challenges - the list is endless. He's killed it everywhere he's been and I don't know why Great Britain didn't play him at six after we smashed the Aussies down there in 2006 - but that's someone else's decision.

We had a really good partnership and we became great friends because of it. I knew what he was doing instinctively, and he knew what I was doing in return. I'll never forget being able to see that big left foot of his step off the line - and when he was at his peak, we'd get so much joy out of it. He had his sulky moments - it wasn't all plain sailing with him! - but that's Leon. We still laugh and joke about it now, and if I'm ever in Bradford or he's over my way, we always make sure we grab a coffee and catch up.

On his day, he was the best in the world - nobody could touch him. That's how good a player he was - and he's an even better bloke. That's probably the best thing I could say about Prycey.

# CHAPTER XIV

# My Dream Team

Full-back is a really tough place to start, probably the toughest position of all to pick if I'm being honest. It comes down to two people really: **Michael Withers** and **Paul Wellens**. When I was 17 and I broke into the first team at Bradford, Mick had just come over from Australia. I didn't know the bloke. He was a quiet, unassuming and skinny bloke, but we became really good friends - it was quite an unlikely combination. He'd left his partner back home in Australia, so it was all a bit alien to him, living in Bradford! I moved in with him way over towards Yeadon, near the airport - and that year we were together produced some of the happiest times of my career.

Mick was an amazing player. He didn't have much about him in terms of size, but when he stepped over the line and onto the field he was an absolute animal. Everyone thought that because he was skinny, he had nothing going for him, but he was so brave, and he won Bradford's Player of the Year award a good few times. His positional sense and tenacity was second to none - and he was just a proper player.

Just above Mick though has to be **Paul Wellens**. We shared the best years of our career together at St Helens, and his game just had this ability to raise everyone else's around him. He made you feel like you had to be at your best, because if you didn't, you shouldn't be at St Helens. I couldn't pick an attribute in the bloke that was at fault, and he just edges my fullback role. He bled for St Helens - literally on a good few occasions -

and you sensed that the club meant everything to him.

On the wing, there were so many to pick from, but one of them is easy to go with in my eyes: **Lesley Vainikolo**. We called him The Volcano and it wasn't hard to work out why. In my opinion he and Jason Robinson are the greatest two wingers to play in Super League.

He broke the mould when it came to being a modern-day winger. In our team, if you gave him the ball anywhere near the try line, nine times out of ten he'd get that ball down. People are often described as freaks in sport but that guy, who looked and played like a prop yet was this incredible winger, was just that: a freak.

His presence on the field was big enough, but what he brought off the field was character. He was untouchable when he was playing, we all know that, but as you'll read elsewhere he was just such a wonderful guy to have around your group. The fans loved him at all the events we had off the field because of his personality and his celebrations, and he became such a key part of our club. He brought the fans close to the club and as a Bradford fan myself, it was nice to see that togetherness he brought.

Les is a fairly straightforward choice but of all the others, I'd have to go with **Tevita Vaikona**. His work rate meant it was like having an extra forward on the field. His try-scoring ratio might not have been as good, but it had to be 'T' for me - although he had loads of competition from the likes of Ade Gardner and people like that.

The wingers might both be from Bradford, but the centres are both St Helens: **Matt Gidley** and **Jamie Lyon**. They were both right centres by trade but I don't care, they're going in: it's my team! When I met Jamie for the first time, I had no idea I was about to share a field every week with the most gifted player I've ever played with. He had the most natural game about him, he had raw speed and he could play so many positions. With a good half-back like Longy feeding him he was untouchable.

In those two years he could sometimes beat teams all on his own. He'd been living in the bush for a couple of years before he came over. When he arrived I saw him do some crazy things that people could only dream of doing - it was insane.

Then there's Gids. What people don't realise is that people always talk about Jamie Lyon and put him on a pedestal of his own. But for us guys that played with Matt, he was just as important to us as a team. His work rate and his passing was massive for a team like ours, and the fact he had a flick pass named after him - the Gidley - tells you all you need to know about his talent.

We all loved him at Saints, particularly the Yorkshire Bus. We adopted him as one of our own. You had Paul Newlove, Kevin Iro and guys like that at Saints in the centres, so there was some huge pressure to follow. That's some task, but he lived up to all those expectations. He was in a very good team - but that wasn't easy.

The halves are tricky ones because I want to put myself in at stand-off! However, I'll have to go with **Henry Paul** and pick players I've played with rather than myself. Henry was a dominating half-back and one that I grew up really looking up to. He was so tenacious and he had such a huge will to win as a player. It's his drive that makes him recognisable to me rather than things like his goal-kicking and his creativity.

He was so much more than an average half-back. He had the body, the speed and the strength, and for a couple of years at Bradford, Henry Paul was the player we all followed in the footsteps of. He set the benchmark when he arrived from Wigan. He led the team and he was potentially the best player in Super League when he was with us. He was inspirational for a lot of young players like myself growing up.

Scrum-half was between three guys - Paul Deacon, Scott Dureau and Sean Long. However, I didn't play enough stand-off with Deacs, so really it's a choice between who I played in the halves with. Scott was super talented, and was a really great guy. We were a brilliant combination together at Catalans and I think he will go on to become a brilliant coach and his attacking abilities were some of the best I've seen. The way he used to square up the line and make it easy for me out the back was great - I loved playing alongside him in France.

But I couldn't leave **Longy** out. He's easily the best scrum-half ever to have played in Super League. By miles. He was a genius on that field. His mind works in ways other people's can't when it comes to rugby. He has more knowledge than any other player and coach in Super League, in my opinion. He can see things and he can also describe it to other people who aren't on his level; and he helped my career more than anyone because I'm not the best organiser, and him doing all that let me do what I do - float around the field and come in and out of the game. That's how I play, like it or lump it, but he helped me be able to do that.

There's not been another half-back like him, and I doubt there ever will be. We always clicked off the field because we were both a bit wild, but beneath all of that is a tender, nice guy and a warm-hearted bloke that I've got a lot of time for.

I initially thought about putting someone else in at prop, but I can't leave **James Graham** out of a team like this. When I was at Saints, Jammer was coming through as a kid, but you just knew that the potential he had was absolutely enormous. The career he's gone on to have in the NRL and with England speaks volumes for the calibre of player he is.

My hooker, much like my full-back, is split between two iconic players - one at Bradford and one at St Helens. On the one hand there's James Lowes because of the influence he had over Bradford during the club's glory years. The tenacity and aggression he had in the game were phenomenal, but the ball service he provided you from dummy-half was magnificent. Playing half-back and getting the ball right in where you want it to be is so underrated by the wider public, and he could do that to perfection.

However, I'd probably have to go with **Keiron Cunningham**. He played with me throughout the best spell of my career and he was like covering three positions for you on the field. Kez had the skill of a half-back, the positional sense of a hooker and the body of a forward! That's no bad thing. Close to the line you just couldn't stop him. Our chain of command at Saints was let Keiron organise, then let Longy follow and I'd be playing behind these two. Sometimes I'd just think, 'wow'. Even after that, there was Paul Wellens behind him - so you can begin to see how we were so successful as a group at St Helens. Having two players on the posts when the attacking team were on the line was a play defences invented because of Keiron and his barge over - he must have got thousands of points for Saints doing that. That's how good he was.

In the other prop position, I've got to go with **Stuart Fielden** because at his peak, he was unstoppable: and he was at his peak for a long, long time. He's a close friend and someone I've got so much time for, but as a player he was ridiculous at times. He nudges out guys like big Joe Vagana at Bradford and Nick Fozzard at St Helens.

The pack is full of leaders - as any good pack should be - and that's epitomised by **Jamie Peacock**, who goes in at the second row. It's difficult to say something about him that hasn't been said because he's such a warrior and he's so highly-regarded - and rightly so. When you hear the name Jamie Peacock it speaks for itself, it's a name that commands respect. We've always got along and he always did things people didn't want to do. When someone doesn't want to carry that tough ball in when the going was tough, he'd do it for you. He didn't do the glorification side of the game, but that's what earned him the respect he has.

On the theme of leaders, JP was close to being joined in the back-row by Gareth Ellis, who did the stuff nobody wanted to do and was such a gentleman off the field. However, having played with him at Bradford and St Helens, as well as for Great Britain, then **Lee Gilmour** gets the nod here.

Loose forward is the Superman, and the Man of Steel: **Paul Sculthorpe**. He's the one guy I think the Australians generally respect for what he's done at international level. We have a lot of guys who are stars and incredible at club level, but Scully is one of the few that's turned it around and done it on the biggest stage too. He beat Australia single-handedly in one game I played with him at Huddersfield, and he is as tough as they come. He's the man, and someone I couldn't leave out of a team like this.

It looks a bit Bradford- and St Helens-heavy, but it's impossible to avoid the fact that they're the two teams where I had most of my success!

## My Dream Team

Paul Wellens (St Helens/Great Britain), Lesley Vainikolo (Bradford), Jamie Lyon (St Helens), Matt Gidley (St Helens), Tevita Vaikona (Bradford), Henry Paul (Bradford), Sean Long (St Helens/Great Britain), James Graham (St Helens/Great Britain), Keiron Cunningham (St Helens), Stuart Fielden (Bradford/Great Britain), Jamie Peacock (Bradford/Great Britain), Lee Gilmour (Bradford/St Helens/Great Britain), Paul Sculthorpe (St Helens/Great Britain).

# CHAPTER XV

We would muck around a lot at Saints, but when we were told to train hard, we always did. Shortly after me joining the club there was a session I'll never forget. Our regular conditioner wasn't in, so it was down to Daniel Anderson to tell us what to do for our cardio and things like that. On this particular day he had us doing what were called 'coat hanger' drills. You'd start on the halfway line at the side of the field, run up to the post, down through the length of the field, under and around the second post and back to where you started - they were gruelling, and I mean it!

Because the conditioner wasn't there, Daniel just punished us. He shouted, 'Go!' - and we went hard. We did a lap, came back and it must have been around 32 seconds and he just muttered, 'Nah, not quick enough', and told us to go again without any rest. We did it again, pushed as hard as we could and he told us we had 10 more to do, and if you don't do them in a certain time you're back in tomorrow on your day off.

All of the Yorkshire Bus looked at each other with a look that screamed we weren't coming all the way back over to St Helens on our day off, and I swear I've never seen Nick Fozzard run as fast - that man was not giving up a day off! Some of the lads were in pieces though. Young Kyle Eastmond and Maurie Fa'asavalu were in a bad, bad way! A lot of people talk about the good times on the field, but some of your best memories are the toughest training sessions you do - and this one involved a session where I was taken to a place physically and mentally that I'd never been to before. I'll never forget it. I did two of these drills and didn't think I could do one more - and we had to do another 10 under the time or we'd be going all the way back along the M62.

We used to burn the candle at both ends and have great nights out, but that was proper team spirit. You can see the pain in each other's eyes and you can see that you need each other to pull you through. That's what gets you camaraderie and makes you tight - and it's why we were so successful, I think.

Players would always do extra bits at Saints to ensure they got to be in peak condition. People like Paul Wellens, Paul Sculthorpe and Jon Wilkin were huge pros and they ensured everyone was on top of their game. Willie Talau would sometimes walk past and up the levels on the machines you were using to try and pain you. These guys were all a similar age to us. It wasn't like we were kids, but no matter who you were, these blokes at St Helens did everything they could to get you at their level - and I think we genuinely responded.

In my time at Saints we had some good people who helped us out, like kit-men and backroom staff. There was Stan Wall and Gibbo, but Ian Harris, who became our kit-man along with Gibbo, is someone I've got to mention.

Ian was a brilliant bloke, but he'd spent most of his early career in the police force before coming on board as a helper with us guys, so he was very disciplined and very tough on people. He didn't get the banter of me and Gilly, given his background. When we found that out, everyone's favourite wind-up merchant Lee Gilmour decided he'd make it his personal goal to torture him. When we got there in a morning, we liked to get there nice and early after a long journey and rustle up some breakfast - just some scrambled eggs on toast. Purposely, because we knew Ian was very sensitive, we'd leave our plates out. We were always going to wash them up, but in our own time, when we were ready!

He couldn't stand the fact we'd left them, so he'd wash them up for us all the time. One morning when he was doing everyone's dishes, Gilly decided to hang on behind everyone else eating so that he could go up to Ian, throw his plate in the sink and say, 'Wash that up for us mate!' - and he'd go spare! It's rude on a different level if you do that with someone you don't know, but we were winding him up, particularly the Yorkshire lads. We had our own little way of winding people up. The physio would spend ages putting the tapes out on the table during training sessions and Foz would just walk in and sweep them all onto the floor - and generally there'd only be me, Gilly and Foz laughing along! We'd always pick them up though afterwards.

Gilly always played well for Saints - really well, in fact - but the way the 2008 season under Daniel Anderson worked out, Paul Sculthorpe forced his way back into the team after spending a fair bit of the year injured. That meant that someone would have to drop out for the Challenge Cup final against Hull FC that year: Fozzard missed out completely and Gilly dropped down to the bench. I think he'd say himself that he had that feeling in the run-up to the final that he would get the nudge out. He'd been playing on the left one week, then on the right, so he was being moved around as it was. When Scully got himself fit for the final, with what he's done in the game, we had a feeling he would almost certainly play. So it was then down to who would miss out in return.

It was understandable when there's a guy like Paul Sculthorpe coming in, but I always remember Gilly being scathing towards Daniel when he found out. He was seething, his head had fully gone! 'I'm not speaking to him again,' he said, referring to Daniel. I know what Gilly's saying to me during the week, saying he didn't deserve to be dropped during the week, and I'd see Gilly blanking Daniel all throughout Wembley week!

Then, would you believe it, only two minutes into the final itself, Scully goes off injured. I think he dislocated his shoulder. It was a different injury to the one he was struggling with anyway. So, Gilly gets thrown on and plays the rest of the first half and plays really well. On this particular day we were overwhelming favourites - having won the cup the last two years in succession - but it was boiling hot at Wembley. Once we got in at half-time - after a whirlwind first-half we led 10-0 - we were all trying to catch our breath. Daniel was coming around giving everyone instructions, speaking to them really calmly and pointing out what he wanted in the second half before turning to Gilly and shouting,

'And you! Get off your fucking outside foot and stop fucking looking at me with that face! You've been doing it all fucking week! Get off your fucking outside foot!'

In coaching terms, that meant that when Gilly was carrying the ball he wanted him to play a little bit squarer at the line, and I was sat next to Gilly as he said it. I've seen the full build-up from both sides: Gilly brushing Daniel off, and I could see the emotion building in the coach all week - and he used half-time in the final to explode! We won the final though, so you can't say it didn't work. But what a time to bring it up, exploding at one of his players in the changing rooms at Wembley!

It was a great final that one, because I managed to fulfil a lifelong dream of scoring a try at Wembley. As a child growing up I had a number of goals I wanted to tick off if I ever became a rugby league player. I remember being at school and while I often hated homework, one day, I was asked to write what my dream moment would be in life - and I knew straight away. Growing up as a rugby fan the Challenge Cup was the pinnacle, nothing would top it - and I still probably think that to this day.

So for once, I'm sat at home as a kid grafting away at my homework and it was all about me being able to play in a Challenge Cup final at Wembley, scoring a try and winning the Lance Todd Trophy for man of the match.

I was lucky enough to win the trophy the year previous, in 2007 against Catalans, but I had never scored that elusive try at such a massive stadium. The story was written as a kid and it was easy to do because I had a passion for rugby, and in 2008 I got the chance to score a try and fulfil my dreams.

We were up by six in the dying stages against Hull, so the game wasn't completely over, and I got a pass down the short side from someone and was able to break through a couple of tackles, run through the line and score the try that sealed the Challenge Cup. The St Helens fans were all behind the posts - over 30,000 of them - where I scored and to be the guy who scored the try that secured another Challenge Cup for St Helens, that was insane. Wilko had scored from a charge-down a few minutes earlier that had edged us in front and we thought we'd won it then before Gareth Raynor pegged one back for Hull, so this was the moment where we all knew we'd done it. And I scored the try! You can't write that - it's magical.

It was a dream come true and something I'd dreamed of since I was nine or ten years old. To celebrate in front of your fans at Wembley by scoring the winning try in a cup final is the pinnacle of my career, it has to be. That single moment was the greatest buzz I've ever experienced and I don't think I ever hit that magical feeling ever again. It was the biggest moment of my career, hands down.

Then we had the most unbelievable trip to Madrid before the play-offs later that year. It was just before we played Leeds because we had a week off owing to being top of the league, so they took us to Spain as a bit of a refresher for the play-offs and the run-in to Old Trafford.

When we got to the hotel we were supposed to be staying in, we all got our stuff together to go chill out by the pool - nothing too serious, nothing too over the top, which was rare for some of us lot at that time! However, we get to the pool and with it being early September-time, we get there and the pool is closed because the summer season had ended at the resort we were staying at!

Straight away, Daniel had a worried look on his face when he found out the pool was closed, because he knew what some of us would probably want to do with our spare time after that! I'll never forget that he said, with the pool being closed, we would enjoy ourselves, but it had to be a 'chill-out, not a wipeout.' I think even he knew that wasn't going to be the case!

We all got together and went off up into the centre of Madrid and had a few beers as a team, nothing too heavy. But then we went right into the middle of Madrid, a really popular area where there were loads of tourists, and we started switching from beers to the big jugs of sangria that you can buy. Each jug was supposed to be for a few people, but some of the lads were buying one each!

Being the idiots we were back then, as we started drinking more and more, we decided to introduce some drinking rules to go along with the fun we were having. They involved stuff like we couldn't call each other by our first names. In fact, we all had other names that night. Mine was Eamonn because I was the chairman of the drinking games and I was in charge and made all final decisions! We couldn't point at each other and we had to drink with our 'wrong' hands. If we got caught out doing any of those, it was downing two fingers' worth of sangria - and we got absolutely bladdered, we were smashed. Being the chairman of the games, it made me even bossier and even more strict on people, which I loved.

But that's just the way we were back then though. We had a good time and although people might have been a bit concerned, it obviously didn't trouble us as we came back and beat Leeds pretty well in the play-offs a week later. That was a full seven days before, so we had time to get it out of our system, and even Eamonn was involved! It was one of the best weekends I've ever had in my life.

It was seriously non-stop and the stuff we got up to was crazy. We all thought we'd continue our running theme of taking the piss out of James Graham by having a James Graham-themed night in the centre of Madrid - and everyone got involved in it, without Jammer initially knowing! We bought a load of ginger wigs and were set to all be dressed up like him, but before we went on the night out, we had a few in Madrid to line our stomachs.

Daniel Anderson was bang up for this night out - and for dressing up like Jammer! - so we were all pumped, and the idea was that we'd be back at the hotel for a certain time so we could retreat to our rooms and get dressed up in the style of the big man to take the piss out of him. Only problem was, we decided to stay out in Madrid and we sort of went with the flow a little bit.

Daniel didn't come in the afternoon and rumour has it he came down into the hotel bar at the agreed time with the ginger wig and the James Graham fancy dress, but he was the only one stood there - we were all out in Madrid, and there's our coach dressed up as James Graham! We heard about it and went back to the hotel and at the agreed time.

Gilly was coming out of contract at the end of that season and he hadn't had any offers. He really wanted to stay at St Helens like most people would have done around that time. Anyway, he was pissed up and feeling pretty full of himself, so he obviously decided to chance his arm and go up to the chairman and say, 'Sort yourself out Eamonn, where's my deal? I've got three huge offers on the table for next year!' - basically trying to call his bluff! He obviously wanted to stay at Saints, but he's calling the chairman tight while he's paying for all of our beers on a trip to Madrid! You couldn't make it up.

Despite all the drinking we did manage to do some eating at one point, and one day we found this tapas bar tucked away in the centre of Madrid. It was the last day before we went home and we went for some food to chill out, ordered some calamari - the best calamari I've had in my life! - but we decided to wash it down with a nice bottle of rosé wine.

That quickly turned into throwing bottles of rosé down our necks and it kicked on from there. I suppose this kind of thing, the whole trip really, would be frowned upon nowadays by some people in the sport. But we were winning games week after week, so our coach didn't mind it and neither did the chairman - especially when we turned up a week later and beat Leeds by 20 points in the play-offs.

When it came to playing and preparing for games our mindset was spot on, and I think if Daniel got even the slightest word that we were out of shape, or drinking to a point that was impacting on our performances, these kind of trips have been stopped.

I just feel very frustrated that we didn't win at least one of the Grand Finals we lost - especially the ones in 2007, 2008 and 2009, when Leeds beat us three times in a row. Throughout the seasons in question we would play brilliantly - we won the League Leader's Shield once or twice I think. We would play really well the week before the Grand Final, but on the big occasion, as a team we were always just a bit off.

In 2007, Leeds played a lot better than us and they definitely deserved it, without a doubt. This is no excuse because Leeds are a great team, but I just feel we needed one more Grand Final success to define us as the best team in Super League. It was just disappointing on a whole other level.

Sometimes we'd turn up and it'd be raining bad at Old Trafford and we were a dry-weather team, and Leeds just managed the conditions better. Personally, I didn't feel like I had my best games in those Grand Finals, which still annoys me and it just felt frustrating that we'd deliver all year - beat Leeds a lot of the time in the season too - before falling short. Credit to them though, they're a champion team, because they peak in the big games.

2008 was devastating. I'd had the best season of my career and I felt going into the game that we had a really good chance - we beat them well the week before - and they got us again! It was a tough one that with it being Daniel's last game in charge. I couldn't have done this book without mentioning losing to Leeds in those three Grand Finals because they stick with me; the Saints boys all talk about it when we meet up to this day.

*Tribute*

# Jon Wilkin

## (St Helens and Great Britain teammate)

I still remember the first time I met Leon. We were 12 years of age and playing junior rugby against each other for the first time. I was playing for East Hull and he was playing for his local team, Queensbury.

The first thing I remember when I saw him run onto the pitch was that apparently this guy was allegedly a child? Give over. I genuinely mean this. He was a similar size back then to what he is now - and that was an intimidating prospect for us kids who were just average size back then! But as a player, he was more skilful than anyone I'd seen at that time playing junior rugby. He was just head and shoulders above the rest of us.

Everything pointed to him having a big future in rugby league, even at such a young age. He absolutely destroyed us every time we played Queensbury and it was no surprise to me that four years later, he would be playing in the first team at Bradford. I really enjoyed playing against him because it was great to watch such a brilliant player in action up close and personal.

For me, the real highlights I have surrounding Leon are just watching him establish himself as a pivotal part of both Bradford and Great Britain teams within a matter of years. I always really respected him as an opponent every time we played against each other for Bradford and St Helens, but I'll never forget a game we had against each other in 2005, Leon's last at Bradford.

One of our players got injured, so I had to jump in at dummy-half and from behind, I just remember Leon absolutely clattering me! Thankfully he'd sign for St Helens the following year and I remember being relieved that I wouldn't have to play against him anymore. This guy that I'd despised from a young age, because he was just so good!

Perhaps the best thing about Leon is how he is as a person. He's one of the funniest and happiest people I've ever met - yet he has an incredibly dry sense of humour to go with it! He's one of the best blokes I've had in my dressing room alongside me, and to have spent so much time together playing is something I'm really proud of. He's an unbelievably talented rugby player with the kind of instincts that you just can't coach. But as well as that, he was a bloke who brought the best out of everyone else around him. He was intelligent, he was a leader and he helped get the best out of people on the field - but off the field, he helped bring everyone closer together.

His biggest strength is probably his biggest weakness though: he cares and worries about anything and everything around him. I think that side of him is perhaps what has got him into strife at certain points throughout his career and life, but the fact he cares so much makes him a brilliant person in my eyes. There's no player who has achieved as much as he has at so many different places, and there is no player I've played with who could do some of the things he did with a rugby ball in his hand.

It was an honour and a privilege to play some of the best parts of my career with him - and I'd definitely say that the time I played with Leon coincided with the most fun I've ever had off the field as a rugby player. He brought an incredible skill-set with him to the Saints and it helped the club flourish.

Leon's most impressive skill for me though was how he perfected the art of arguing! He could argue, believe me - but he could also instigate trouble and then disappear into the night! We called him 'The Firestarter' at Saints and with good reason, because he'd put kindling under a bubbling argument, light it and run a million miles! When it exploded, he'd be nowhere near it all. He'd be the chief puppeteer alongside his two mates, Nick Fozzard and Lee Gilmour. He could bubble things away under the surface and when it kicked off, you'd just see a flash of training kit heading out of the door. I'm sure he's told plenty of those stories himself.

But another thing he also taught me was the fine art of how to dress for training. We used to have a Leon Pryce-shaped scale of how ready Leon Pryce was for training, judged on what he would have on his body. It all related to the number of pieces of equipment he had on. He'd drive over from Yorkshire at 7:30am and when he got out of that car, we could tell where he was mentally by what he was wearing. If he had the bare minimum - I'm talking shorts, a t-shirt and trainers - then we knew he would be on fire in training that day and he'd be almost untouchable.

However, if he turned up with a hoodie, tracksuit bottoms, a padded jacket and a big wooly hat, we knew that it was staying on for the rest of the day and you could guarantee training wouldn't be Leon's favourite thing that day! Leon's attitude and application for training was directly related to the amount of kit he had on at any one time. We found that out pretty quickly when he came to Saints!

But that's the thing about Leon. We used to laugh seeing him wear all this clobber, but underneath it, he was fiercely competitive. He's a bit of an enigma in the way that he didn't necessarily have to be on it to be world-class. He might not have been 100 per cent focussed one day, but he could still be incredible if he wanted to be. That's a pretty special talent to have.

Obviously he travelled over to Saints with Nick Fozzard and Lee Gilmour and together, they were a right crowd. They made it easy for the rest of us though, because you didn't have to talk as they'd be prattling on with their own conversations, winding people up and generally making it fun to be at training. We didn't have to contribute too much! Leon was the smartest out of the three in that he knew how to play people better than anyone else. He would start with hammering someone and he knew who he had in the crosshairs - more often than not it would be young kids like Paul Clough or the Aussie guys. They'd make the lives of some of the lads a living hell!

He was a big voice, but that meant when it came to anything like social functions and nights out, he was great to have around. He'd make us all laugh and chuckle all the time. Sometimes we would laugh at him though. We'd go out and, being rugby players like we are, we'd have a few pints and enjoy ourselves.

But while we're drinking pints, Leon would be sat with some sort of fruity concoction with a straw in and that would be a constant source of amusement for us. He'd always say he wanted something to quench his thirst, so he'd get a pink or orange cocktail! He was the life and soul of the party all the time, but you could tell he's desperately close to his family too. He's a proper family man and it's obvious he's just a good bloke.

Anyone who played with Leon will say they can't help but love the guy. Leon Pryce is an utterly crazy man, but everyone who came across him will probably love him forever more - especially at St Helens. He left a real impact on the place and he was great for us both on and off the field. It's the times away from the rugby pitch which I will really remember about Leon though. He's a great bloke who cared a lot about what he did, he loved his teammates and he was a major part of the sustained success the club managed to enjoy.

For that, as a friend, a teammate and a peer, I would just like to thank him.

# CHAPTER XVI

*In July of 2008 I was involved in an off-field incident which ended up going through the courts. I pleaded guilty to an assault charge and was sentenced to 100 hours of community service. Here is my explanation as to what happened and why it did.*

The whole case was around two years from start to finish and it obviously was really drawn out, which is the way it is I guess with the courts. Amazingly, while it was all happening, I was playing my best rugby, as I've said elsewhere. But just like it was all those years ago, rugby was again an escape, to be honest, and it was helpful - like it was all those years ago with the earlier court case I had to contend with as a young kid.

I'm not really sure how much detail I can go into really when it comes to the incident itself, but all I know is that I was sticking up for a friend, my best friend in fact, in Stu. In hindsight though, it was pretty stupid, wasn't it? I was a high-profile rugby player - an international rugby player at that time too - who was playing the best stuff of his career, so perhaps I shouldn't have got myself involved with it all.

But I'm not like everyone else. I'm not one to think that because there's stuff in the papers about you or there might be a bit of negative press that it makes you a bad person, because it doesn't in my opinion.

So I'm not a clean-cut, squeaky clean bloke. I value my friendship with certain people higher than whatever rubbish comes out about me in a newspaper and if that lets people who don't know me interpret me in a bad light, then it is what it is.

Those who know me know what I stand for, and on that night, I stood for what I thought was right - defending a friend who needed some help.

He was going through a really rough time was Stu, and he was going through a separation with his wife at the time and it was messy, there was no getting away from that. And at the time when he truly needed me, his real hour of need, I was there for him and I wouldn't have had it any other way. It was one of those situations where thinking about rugby and my profile in the public limelight went out of the window, because I wanted to do what I thought was right. If that got me in trouble, then so be it. I'm not embarrassed by it and I'm not ashamed by it whatsoever.

It's the complete opposite of the first court case earlier in my life. It still embarrasses me now that I did what I did and I ended up going through the courts and almost going to prison.

But this didn't embarrass me at the time and it doesn't now. I was ashamed of what I did in the nightclub in Bradford, but I'm not ashamed of this and I'm not afraid to talk about it whatsoever. I did it because I stuck up for my best friend. Sat here now in my mid-30s, I'm accepting of the fact we shouldn't have done what we did - and even that night, I remember saying to Stu that it would have been best if we'd left the place where it all happened and not let it get as messy as it did. But do I regret being stood by his side? Not a chance.

He said he didn't want to go anywhere because he wanted to see what the situation was with his wife, and he wasn't budging - so that was my mind made up, I was there to help him and see him through an incredibly rocky time in his life. I had the choice to leave my best mate, hang him out to dry and potentially let something happen to him. I chose to stand by him. I'm pretty confident that 99 per cent of people reading this would think it was the right thing to stick by someone who has stood by them in return when times have been tough.

In hindsight, I should have dragged him away from the whole incident, but I know what he's like - it wasn't going to happen. Of course I'm not happy about what happened and I'm not happy that my name was chucked all over the press as a result of it, but I'm at least content now looking back that I helped a friend who was in need.

It completely messed Stu's career up. I got to keep on playing and St Helens were good with me, but Warrington ripped up his deal and his career was effectively over, despite him being an absolutely brilliant player at that time. I'm not trying to make myself out to be some sort of hero here, but you've got loyalties and morals in life. Some people are loyal to their image, to money, whatever - my loyalties lie with my friends and family. If that makes me look like a prick, well so be it. You can't read something about someone in a newspaper and pretend you know them more than anyone, because you don't unfortunately.

I've spoken about how great Bradford were throughout the first court case earlier in my career and the same is applicable to St Helens with this whole mess. They were absolutely awesome in how they handled it and, perhaps more importantly, how they supported me from start to finish. It was just a stupid thing that should have never happened, but Saints were great with it all.

People have asked me since whether I feared the worst about going to prison, given how close I was the first time, and I had this blot on my card from the past, but I honestly wasn't. I knew it wasn't anywhere near as bad as the first incident - in context it was far less. I was a lot more optimistic that prison wasn't going to be a realistic option because I saw everything that happened and I knew the full story. In my opinion it wasn't worthy of anything, but we're sports stars aren't we - maybe they wanted to make an example out of us.

But again it's just so stressful for your wife, your parents, your children and your close friends. But also for your club and your sponsors. They don't want to see their name associated with press like this. Again, the fact you're being talked about and gossiped about around Bradford, you just don't need it. It was a moment that changed how I socialise in and around where I live - to the point where I tried to do most of my socialising around my best friends and in private.

I don't go out that much, and I don't need to because I don't need the gossip that lingers after stuff like this. The first case changed me as a person and this one probably had more of an impact on how I lived my life in terms of going out. Why bother anymore?

The person I remember it being really tough for was my mum. She's not the best at communicating and expressing how she feels half of the time anyway, and she had to go through all this court fiasco again, just a few years after watching her son be told he might be going to prison. It was a real strain on her and it stressed her out which has a knock-on effect to everyone else. But it's me who caused it. I've got to deal with it.

I know people will think I'm being apologetic here, but in this day and age, there's not as much of a stigma attached to a male being depressed as what there was when this kind of stuff happened - and it did depress me. I wasn't a happy person for a long, long time. In rugby I was loud and brash, but away from that I was constantly beating myself up and I was a very unhappy person with my life.

I know that a lot of people only see the glamorous side of professional sport and being a rugby league player, and they think that we all get paid a fortune and are superstars, but in reality, we get quite a modest income for what we put our bodies through. It's not massive, it's not like being a footballer, and 95 per cent of players that have been in the game have to go into another walk of life and do something else when they retire. They can't just sit around for the rest of their lives, play golf and drink coffee. We all have to go to work and the pressures you put on yourself with the media, and it being such a male-driven, macho sport, you're taught from a very young age that you're not supposed to show pain or emotion.

If you're hurt on the pitch or away from the field then you were expected to stand up and, dare I say it, act like a man, as people would often say way back then. You've got to live with being smashed in tackles and being hurt and you take it with you through life. I remember seeing people get knocked out and getting stitches on the field, playing on with injections in their bones and breaking bones - things you do to play. It became quite apparent over the last couple of years when we've been talking more and more about mental health. But the reason it's so prominent in rugby league is that we're taught not to talk about emotion or show that we're hurt.

If you cry, you're perceived as a wimp, or at least you were. As men, we're not meant to be that way and in rugby league it's magnified 1000 times, so that brings pressure. Rugby league lads have to deal with that pressure and they do so in different ways. Some deal with it really well, others really struggle. Some go on drinking binges and do things off the field that the normal public don't understand - it's like a release. If you're not involved, you don't really get it and I understand that. It's going out of the game now thankfully because it's more professional, but it's changed a lot from when I first started.

You still need a release as a player and you still need time away from being a rugby player and being this macho man who isn't supposed to show any pain. We're starting to get the message out now that it is okay to talk and it is okay to tell people how you're feeling. The acceptance there that you can talk now is really refreshing and really heartening for the sport and the world.

I never really felt that pressure on a day-to-day basis, I always seemed to put it on myself more than anything. The pressure is naturally on a bit more on occasions, like when you're coming off contract at the end of a season, when you're injured, or when you don't get along with the coach – there are lots of different factors. I think when you're successful you put it on yourself a bit more anyway, I know I did. There's no bigger pressure than the one you put on your own shoulders, but as I say, we all deal with it in different ways and I'd be the first to admit that there have been times where I've not been all that great in dealing with it from time to time. But you've got to learn to deal with it as a professional and that's quite tough really.

Luckily, rugby helped to take it all off my shoulders. But driving home on those long journeys on the M62 to and from St Helens, I couldn't help but think about whether what the press was saying was right. You start to doubt yourself and in turn you become, without putting too fine a point on it, depressed with your life. I've learned to ignore the press though, because it just drags you down. I know I'm not a bad person and I know who I am. I've been pre-judged in some parts of my life for stuff like this, and while I take full responsibility for everything I've done, and I'll take everything that comes my way, nobody truly knows who I am by what they read.

Looking back on it all, it was a small, stupid incident that could have been dealt with a lot better, in my opinion. It's one of those things that shouldn't have got as far as it did.

# CHAPTER XVII

At the start of 2009, after Daniel left and went home, we went down the route of appointing another Australian as Mick Potter came into the club. His first day involved a story I'll never forget - yet again involving the one and only Nick Fozzard! We had a cupboard in the inner sanctum of the club which was big enough to hold a human being as big as Foz in - you can guess where this is going - and it had all the medical stuff in. So we decided that we'd strip Foz naked, tie him to a chair so he couldn't move and then put him in the cupboard and shut the door! We taped his mouth up and everything to make it look like he'd been captured and then when Mick Potter came in and opened the cupboard on his first day, what does he see - a big naked prop forward screaming with his mouth taped up! Thankfully Mick got over that, but it definitely scared him to death, I saw it on his face!

That was Foz all over. We used to have a skeleton in the medical room like you see in doctors' surgeries, and he used to just randomly grab the hips and start dancing and stupid stuff like that! Nobody knew how to take him, but he was so funny.

When I first came through Bradford's academy system, I worked really hard and did lots of things away from the field to make sure I could become a top player. I'd make a lot of sacrifices, such as not going out with my mates when I was 18 or 19, which was huge. My mates would go out drinking and do what teenage lads generally did, but I was out running at 5am in the morning and late at night to be good enough.

I put a lot into it, but back then, it wasn't as professional as it is nowadays. I might have slacked off with my training sometimes and just made sure I was ready for games, but with the professionalism not being as high, I got away with it, to be honest. That became who I was and it became part of me. I just wasn't a great trainer. I liked the rugby and skills side of things, but not the weights and the fitness stuff. It all bored me even though I knew it was useful. I've got a short attention span and if I don't enjoy something, I won't really immerse myself in it. That was just the way I was. I would never advise my son to be like that now, and I wouldn't say it was right, but I relied too much on my talent and it got me through all my career.

Rugby is a game full of lunatics like you wouldn't believe, and I think you've got to be a lunatic to want to actually play rugby in the first place. Fozzard is definitely up there with the craziest people I've ever met and he's one of the best blokes to have in a group of players and have on your team. On a day-to-day basis, you never knew what you would get from that bloke. One day he was goading me to throw a dart at him. I kid you not, this is the kind of bloke we're dealing with here. He was egging me on and begging me to throw this dart at him and I just thought I would to see how close I could get it to him without it actually hitting him. But I'm not the best darts player, sadly, and my aim was off. It ended up going straight into his leg!

He's such a genuinely nice person though. You would struggle to find anyone that would say a bad word about him off the field - he's a proper gentleman.

People used to tell me they didn't know how we could do that journey every day, going to St Helens, but by the end of it we ended up having a special bond between us all. It gave us a connection that you couldn't really forge with anyone else, we're all still good friends now. People like Foz stopped playing around the turn of the decade.

One weekend, we'd been out in St Helens after playing a game - I can't remember who it was against - but it was definitely on a Friday night. We were out on the drink and while everyone gets a bit loose when they've had a few beers, Gilly gets even looser, if that makes sense!

He's a hilarious drunk, but in this instance he bumped into a lass in a bar in St Helens and sent her flying. All her mates were quite rowdy and upset about it, but it was nothing more than an accident, because Gilly was in a bit of a state by this point. Anyway, to be fair to them, they managed to all move on and forget about it and so did we, so we went off enjoying the rest of our night, thinking nothing else of it. It looked like it would kick off for a split second though.

That was until training on the Monday, however. Before that there were rumours swirling round, started by someone that this woman's fella was a gangster or a real hardman. So we were training at a place called Ruskin and it was a real secure complex, and suddenly, some geezer started walking across the complex and making his way to the field we were all training on. It's cut-off, and if someone is in there who you don't know, something bad is generally going to happen - and I could see that Gilly had a real worried look on his face.

A couple of the lads must have seen it and found out what had gone on so everyone's suspecting Gilly has pissed someone off big time over the weekend, but eventually, he wandered off and disappeared. Tuesday came around and we were training as normal again, but I could feel something wasn't right when we were warming up, as all the lads were sniggering and giggling like a bunch of kids. Straight away my senses pricked up to something going on, but I naturally forgot about it when we got into training.

The session finished and we had a bit of a stretch off, all laid down on the grass. I looked over to the bushes on the edge of the complex and saw a different guy start marching over to us with a hood up. Straight away I knew it was dodgy, as he had a baseball bat under his arm, and he shouts, 'Oi! Which one of you lot is Lee Gilmour? I'm going to fucking hurt you!'

'Shit!' That was literally the first word that came into my mind. What has he done now? By this time, I stood up and Matt Gidley and Maurie Fa'asavalu went over to this guy to try and calm him down, as we're all looking around trying to work out what the hell is happening. 'No, I won't fucking calm down,' this guy says. 'I want to know who Lee fucking Gilmour is because he's getting it and I'm gonna hurt him!'

This time, he drops the baseball bat after saying that and he pulls out a gun - and not a toy one: an actual gun. You might think it was a fake on instinct, but when this guy pulled the gun out, he let off a couple of shots to make sure we all knew it was real and he was serious. 'What the actual fuck is happening,' I'm thinking. I turned left and - I remember this as clear as day, my life descended into slow motion - I have genuinely never been as frightened in all my life. Surely to God this guy, whoever he is, knows that Lee Gilmour is white and not a big black guy. 'I am not Lee Gilmour, this guy can't think I'm Lee Gilmour,' that's all I kept telling myself as I'm sprinting away as fast as I can to avoid some maniac with a gun.

'It can't be me! Please don't let him shoot at me. I'm so scared!'

At this point though, I was in my peak playing years, so I was seriously quick. So I backed myself to get away from this guy and I was pumping my legs as fast as they went, probably because some geezer was waving a gun around!

As I look right, I see a couple of the youngster lads, like Jamie Ellis and Chris Dean, trying to get into the facility at Ruskin and pleading for someone to open this door that was locked. 'Let me in,' they're screaming - and I didn't blame them for nearly being in tears and having faces of absolute fear. It was all in slow motion and I kept running. I remember telling myself, 'Do not stop, Leon! Run!'

Anyway, I clocked this tree which was about as tall as the secure wall around the Ruskin complex - it was about 12 foot tall - and I fancied myself to get up that tree and hop over the wall. However, as I started to realise I couldn't reach the top of the wall, I began to panic even more. I turned around to see what my next option was, because I didn't know where this guy was who was wielding a gun, but as I turned around, I saw all the lads laid on the floor, rolling around in fits of laughter. Bastards!

It was a massive set-up and they got me a beauty. I was as white as I could possibly be with fear and I went back over to try and find out who knew, and it turns out Gilly himself didn't! Although in true Lee Gilmour fashion, I asked him why he didn't run away and he just nonchalantly said, 'I knew it wasn't a real gun, I could tell by the shape of the handle on it.' Whatever!

Gilly was actually trying to blend into a group to make sure he didn't get shot at, but that was the scariest thing I've ever been involved in throughout my whole life, not just my career - but it's easily the funniest thing, by far!

It was only supposed to wind Gilly up, but the lads who set it up decided not to tell a few more of us too, which was good of them! It was the Yorkshire Bus who didn't get told, I learned, as Keiron Cunningham had sorted it with Mick Potter - and it was Keiron's brother-in-law who had been roped in to be the bloke with the gun threatening to kill Lee Gilmour!

That was around the time Gilly was coming to the end of his contract at St Helens. I think it ran out the following year, and there was a bit of a dispute between what he had been offered and what he wanted, as I recall. Anyway, he confided in one of the lads and, I'm still not sure whether he was joking or not to this day, but he said he was going to put a transfer request in with the chairman. I knew Gilly definitely didn't want to leave, but it was a bit of bravado that got out of hand.

We all found out one way or another, and on the bus on the way back from the Challenge Cup final that year, we were all buzzing and James Graham decided to wind Gilly up a bit. He started singing, 'He puts his transfer in, his transfer out; in, out, in, out, shake it all about. Ohhh Gilly Gilly Gilly!' The whole bus was singing it and you could see Gilly was hating it, because all the attention and spotlight was on him and he really doesn't like that!

We eventually got back to St Helens after the final and, as the guy christened 'The Firestarter' by everyone, I thought I'd live up to the billing. I got on the microphone and started singing the song we were all singing on the team bus. Bearing in mind this was with a few members of the public this time and not just the team, everyone was cracking up - except one man.

'He puts his transfer in, his transfer out...' reverberated around the club we were in and it got louder and louder and Gilly's face was like thunder. You can see he was getting angrier and angrier and he was actually stood next to Jon Wilkin with a beer in his hand while we're all singing - and he booted Wilko in the leg to shut him up! Wilko didn't know what to say because, as we know, it wasn't his fault it had started was it - it was all The Firestarter's doing! I think eventually we all were convinced by Gilly to drop it, because he didn't want the chairman getting wind that he was joking about putting a transfer request in. If he had, he'd have probably been off whether he liked it or not!

Under Daniel, we used to pull each other's leg all the time. In fact, we did it when Mick Potter was there plenty of times too and it went straight over his head more often than not. When we used to watch our video reviews back on a Monday morning, they were ordinarily quite good to watch back at Saints. Sometimes if you're struggling for form or you lose the weekend before, the video room is not where you want to be.

It's like watching a horror film at times, but throughout the glory years at Saints, we were winning most weeks so we ended up just watching brilliant rugby back - and we'd let Daniel know about it! He used to pick a move where we'd scored a brilliant try and basically tell us this was what he wanted all the time, but as he did and the passes were strung together on video, we'd all go, 'Oh! Oh! Oh! Ohhhhhh!' - basically patting ourselves on the back and launching into a massive round of applause as the final player in the move put the ball down over the line! We were joking and everyone knew we were joking, including the coach - but Fozzard was the man who was often at the heart of it, trying to wind everyone up!

But when Mick Potter took over after Daniel, we didn't stop doing it. So we'd have a video review after a win and do exactly the same again. 'Oh! Oh! Oh! Ohhhhhh!' But Mick wasn't sure why we were so cocky and arrogant, as we're all standing up applauding each other! He didn't know we were messing around, but we carried on with it and one morning, he told us we were in love with ourselves and it was embarrassing!

But Potter used to get annoyed by loads of stuff - and sometimes, I'd be on the same page as him. James Graham and Sia Soliola used to have this awful routine where they'd clap at random intervals and see who would be the last to do it, but it was so, so annoying! Mick would start to speak and one of them would clap, the captain would talk up and the other would clap, and it would wind so many of us up - but none more so than Mick Potter.

Sometimes players can have problems sleeping after games, which is only natural. Carly had gone away, up to Center Parcs for the weekend or something like that, and I'd got some sleepers off a teammate to relax me while I was at home after a game on a Friday night. But it turned out they weren't sleepers. They were sedative tablets for psychiatric patients! Don't ask me how this teammate of mine got them, but he had them! I didn't know, obviously, so I woke up in the morning and I just couldn't get my head in a place where I could properly wake up.

I was supposed to be training on the Saturday morning after a game, but I just physically couldn't get out of bed. My head was in bits, a right mess, and all over the place. Paul Sculthorpe had actually lent me his car this weekend, as it happened, because mine was in for repair - and he had this massive Range Rover. It was a beauty.

He needed something doing to it and I knew a garage in Bradford that worked specifically on these kind of cars, so he agreed to give it to me for the weekend, get some side skirts put on the motor and then return it to him on the Monday. But I'd had these sleeping tablets to get me off after a game on the Friday night and somehow, I don't know how and I still can't remember, I've scratched the car, all the alloys and I've actually bumped it in the process of getting to training. I genuinely still can't remember a thing about it to this very day. The car ended up breaking down on the way to St Helens, just before Birch service station. I've pulled over into the hard shoulder, put my chair into recline mode and because I was so tired, I've gone back to sleep on the middle of the motorway because I've had these sedatives that are supposed to be for psychiatric patients!

Anyway, the police must have pulled up behind me, because I heard a tap on the window and they obviously asked me what the hell I was doing sat laid asleep on the middle of the M62. They quickly worked out who I was and they told me that they were going to have to impound the car because it was just a complete and utter mess - bearing in mind this is Paul Sculthorpe's car.

I obviously had to get home somehow, so I rung my old man and he drove along to the middle of the M62, picked me up and took me back home. All this time I'm trying to get to training to do my job, but my head is so off the pace that I'm not thinking straight whatsoever. I went back home and got in my little Peugeot 307 and all I can remember is that when I finally got near the training ground at St Helens, my eyes started to close. It wasn't like a blink either. It was my eyes shutting because I was going into a deep sleep. Looking back, it's as scary as hell to recall. All I remember then is that I went into the central reservation on a dual-carriageway and then into the wire things that separated the two sides of the road. I scraped all the side of the car and it was in a right state, but somehow I managed to get to training - although it had all finished by the time I got there because I'd been up and down the M62 all morning.

The first person I saw was Scully who said, 'Where's my car lad?' and my honest reply was, 'I don't know.' I genuinely didn't. 100%. I had no clue whatsoever. It was like my brain had been erased somewhere along the line. These sedatives had done the trick and they'd wiped me out and all Scully kept asking me was where his car was and I couldn't answer him. That was the conversation all afternoon and, as it happened, I was staying in St Helens because we had a team do that night, so it all rolled over into the evening - understandably so, I guess, given how Scully didn't know what had happened to his swanky Range Rover!

When I woke up in the morning after this social with the Saints lads, my head had obviously cleared and I started to be able to piece things together about the last 24 hours of my life. But it wasn't until I found a ticket in my pocket detailing that the car had been impounded when I started to realise what had happened. I rushed back home as quick as I could, hurried off to get the car and paid someone a bit of money to get it all fixed up. It was a pretty expensive weekend, that one!

Eventually though, things have to change in rugby - and nothing lasts forever. Gilly moved on, Keiron retired, Longy left, and the iconic squad all started to go their own way. Daniel Anderson had gone, Mick Potter came and went and I started to look around eventually and realise that my time was beginning to end there, too. When I signed for Saints I knew from the off that I didn't really want to move my children and my family out of Bradford.

The bonds I built with the lads I travelled with last forever, and of course it helps that we had such a good laugh when we were travelling over. Even though it's a bit of a pain in the arse travelling, they were still the best days. God knows what Baloo must have thought at times though, we were all mental and acting up all the time and he could be a bit miserable!

But the way my time at St Helens came to an end, being basically on the shelf for a long time with injury, was awful. But I'd learned to accept by the time it ended that it's part and parcel of rugby and players do get injuries. I don't regard it as a particularly bad time of my life, more a learning curve for me as a person, who was only around the age of 30 and still, in life terms at least, fairly young.

I went through a bad time off the field and I remember playing against Wakefield in 2010 and playing the best I've ever played in a one-off game - and I mean that, I was on fire. Every single thing I did went right, every touch, every kick and every pass created a try and it was just one of those days where everything seemed to click.

During that game towards the back end, I took the ball in, dummied and a Wakefield player had hold of my legs really tight so I couldn't move - so I kept hold of the ball to go down and Sam Obst tackled me in such a way - accidentally, I've got to say - that all the pressure went straight onto my neck and I could feel my spine click all the way up into the back of my head. Straight away I knew that wasn't right because I'd never felt that happen before.

Anyway, I came off and thought nothing of it, because I was fine shortly after, but then the following week we were playing Warrington away and it still wasn't right and I was getting pain in my shoulder blades all the time. Literally most nights were spent with Carly rubbing my shoulders to try and ease this horrible pain, so I knew something was up almost immediately. It was during the build-up to playing Leeds in the Challenge Cup semi-final when all this was happening, and I knew I was playing in that game no matter what, because we had to beat them - especially with it being Leeds!

However, they eventually made me go for a scan because this pain wasn't easing in my shoulder and it wouldn't shift - it wasn't right, which was obviously worrying with such a big game coming up. I wasn't really sure what to expect going into this scan, but it turned out that it wasn't my shoulder as I thought, I'd actually perforated a disc in my neck and took a chip out of one of the discs, so straight away I knew I was in trouble. I missed that game against Leeds, which we lost, and it put me out of action for four months in all, which was tough to deal with because it was coming up to the most crucial part of the season. There's nothing you can do about it except try and come back fitter and stronger, but just as I'd worked my way back from that, I got another setback at the start of 2011.

During pre-season you'd change surfaces all the time with the fields being so boggy and unpredictable in England. One week you'd be on rock-hard training grounds if they were frozen and the next you'd be playing in mud if they were boggy after loads of rain - and when you throw in some warm-weather training on lush playing fields, your body can sometimes find it tough to contend with.

You're always looking for dry surfaces, but surfaces like AstroTurf were giving my back and knee real grief because my body couldn't get used to what it was playing on. I always hated training on those AstroTurf surfaces. I wasn't in the best shape I'd ever been in too, admittedly, but I'd developed this problem where my pubic bone was really sore all the time, so I went in for a steroid injection to get rid of the inflammation and I was told to rest up by the doctors. I had a couple of weeks off and we played Catalans away and I stepped off my left foot in the first few minutes and just felt this twang: my adductor had snapped off the bone, clean as a whistle.

That put me out for another 12 to 14 weeks, so that's well over half a season again really. I think that, all told, I played about five minutes of competitive rugby between July 2010 and July 2011 with this neck injury and the torn adductor. But I moved on, worked hard and I got back fit. I played in all the pre-season friendlies going into 2011 and I thought I was on the right track, but I refused to let it sit on my mind and my thinking. You don't take stuff like that too seriously. Once the doctor gives you the all-clear you forget all about it - but with the neck injury, I did wonder if I would play again. Obviously players have had to retire or worse through neck injuries, so when you get told what's happened you do fear the worst and think about what's going to happen next.

I missed out on some big nights and some big games and among them was the last ever game at Knowsley Road, and that was a wild night that I bet even just being there was special - but I watched that game at home. Looking back, I wish I had gone, but it was great to see Keiron Cunningham score the last ever try at that ground.

But I've had that many good experiences in my career that I won't nitpick on the odd ones that have been bad. I've played in so many finals I can't keep count and I've ticked off so many things, so I'm lucky to have done everything I've done. It was about this time of my career where I began to sit back and realise this, rather than worrying about the ones I was missing. Up until the age of 28 or 29, I'd had injuries that were only in and around the end of the season, so that meant I could have operations at the end of the year or play through the pain for a few weeks before I could rest up - but these ones were awful. It made me much more sympathetic for players who had to miss large chunks of seasons with knocks.

The club brought Royce Simmons in after Mick Potter left to go to Bradford and I was one of the last of the old guard who were left from the so-called glory years. Sean Long had gone, Keiron Cunningham had retired, Paul Sculthorpe had gone, and so on. The players were outspoken and there was a lot of player power in the dressing room - which isn't always a bad thing in my opinion - and Royce tried to change that philosophy.

Coming towards the end of my time at Saints, I didn't help myself as much as I could have done. If I'd taken care of myself better off the field in coming back from my injury, and tried a little harder to get on with the coach, then maybe we could have renegotiated in relation to me staying at Saints. But that, along with missing 14 weeks of playing, along with having a new coach, means you miss a good part of the season and by the

Mine and Carly's wedding day.

All smiles
on my
wedding
day.

Joking around on my wedding day...

...before looking all serious!

A great family shot of me, Carly, William and Lily...

...and another!

Right after we'd won the 2006 Grand Final - and the treble - at St Helens.
(Dave Williams RLPHOTOS.com)

With the Saints fans after winning a Challenge Cup semi-final.
(Dave Williams RLPHOTOS.com)

Celebrating scoring the winning try in the 2008 cup final...
(Dave Williams RLPHOTOS.com)

...and all smiles with the cup! (Dave Williams RLPHOTOS.com)

Celebrating another big win during my time at St Helens.
(Dave Williams RLPHOTOS.com)

Just after becoming the first Englishman to play for Catalans Dragons.
(Dave Williams RLPHOTOS.com)

With the legend, 'The Beaver', Steve Menzies during our time together at Catalans.

Me and my beautiful wife, Carly.

Me and the wife enjoying the sunshine!

My two beautiful kids, William and Lily.

A Saints reunion with some of the 2006 squad: what a team!

A much more recent photo of the Yorkshire Bus enjoying a quiet drink!

Happy times as a Hull FC player. (Dave Williams RLPHOTOS.com)

Not sure what face Gilly is pulling here!

All the boys looking dapper!

Another of my best mates in rugby league: Hull's Danny Houghton.

The man they call 'Mint': super Danny Houghton.

Back as a Bull for 2017. (Dave Williams RLPHOTOS.com)

time I'd come back to play, I had already agreed to move on.

Looking back, I wish I had handled it in a better way and maybe tried a bit harder with the coach, but I'm a hard-headed person who is sometimes too stubborn.

I'd been out all that time injured, and during that period I had planned to go back to Bradford in 2012. I basically negotiated a deal myself to go back to the Bulls, which I was happy about and I was content with. But during my last year at Saints, I wanted to make sure legally if it was on the money and it was all properly done. So I spoke to a lawyer, Richard Cramer, who ran through it all for me.

Basically I just wanted him to dot the i's and cross the t's, and he agreed to do it straight away, because he's a good bloke, is Richard. The next day he rang me back, and I was expecting him to say the contract was sweet, and we were good to go - back to Bradford, happy days. No travelling, back at my first club and the one I never really wanted to leave in the first place, sorted.

However, he said that he wanted to give me a bit of advice and he wanted me to take a step back and have a think about this Bradford deal, because he had been made aware Catalans had expressed their interest in me - and they were really keen. Richard said he'd had contact from Trent Robinson at Catalans, and while I didn't really fancy going to France - my heart was set on going back to Bradford - I thought I'd be stupid to ignore offers from elsewhere, even if I was fairly certain I was heading back to Odsal.

# **Nick Fozzard**

## (St Helens and Great Britain teammate)

*Dangerous Darkness.*

That's one of my many nicknames for Leon Pryce and it quickly caught on. Before we went out to play when we were together at St Helens I would always say to him, 'Be dangerous' - and he always was.

For me, Leon is one of the greatest stand-offs the game has ever seen - not just Super League. He is an opposition's nightmare, without a shadow of a doubt - especially when we were on a roll at Saints, which we often were.

He's got incredible footwork. He's big, he's strong and he's fast. At his peak he had everything. His football brain is phenomenal and when you put him together with Sean Long in the halves at Saints at the start of 2006, you had what I would consider to be the best half-back partnership I've ever played with - and the best I've ever seen for that matter.

On the field, Leon had so many good traits about him and in his game. He could throw a great long pass, a brilliant short one and he'd also not be afraid of going to the line and taking a knock in order to put a man through a gap. Not to mention that he's a brilliant decision maker and, under pressure, he always delivered.

But I also love how that even though he's a great individual player that can turn a game on its head all by himself, he was a player who made others play well around him to boot. He's a team player - and that's a great asset to have.

Make no mistake about it though, he's fiery - very fiery - and he likes to be on top of his game every single time he plays, and he has high expectations of his mates around him as a result of it. That can irk some people, I guess, but I love that - I love that he's a bit nasty. He's not proud of it, I know, but for a back to have a bit of nastiness in them is great in my opinion - especially a half-back. It fires me up and it's good to have it in you when it's really needed.

Like the time he took out Kevin Sinfield and Jamie Lyon at different points of his career with terrible high shots to the head. They were both off the ball incidents too and I know he's not proud of them! But for me, I love that he can do that, I love that he can think like that and he has it in him.

He's ultra loyal and he will always back his mates up, no matter what. He won't be intimidated in any situation. He'll stand his ground and he expects that from both his teammates and his friends. If he ever thought I wasn't playing as tough as was needed he would go crazy with me and call me all the names under the sun!

And then I would fire up and go absolutely crazy! He got the best out of me as a player. He annoyed me at times, but that was what I needed sometimes - like when we played Wigan once and he was screaming at me to run harder, calling me all the names under the sun - and when I heard him, I saw red!

I demanded the ball in absolute fury and anger and ran at Stuart Fielden, knocking him out cold! Then I walked straight up to Leon, slammed the ball in his chest and just asked, 'What? You mean run hard like that, Leon?'

He sheepishly replied, 'Yes, Foz, just like that.'

Rugby league is a tough, cruel game, and to be the best you need to have a certain ruthless edge about you - not all the time, but on occasions it's really needed - and Leon definitely has that in him. It's not just in a game when you want it, it's in training when you need to be tough. You need to be tough to keep going through the pain and learn to make the right decisions when you are fatigued and things like that.

I love how he takes it upon himself to take responsibility for things on the field. If his team were ever on the back foot, he would take the ball off the cuff like a forward and get us moving again. He'd use his footwork and his size to get us back on top - he could do things like that.

But more importantly, Leon Pryce the player was great - and Leon Pryce the person was great, great fun.

Leon, Gilly and myself were crazy when we all got together. Travelling over from Yorkshire every day for a few years, there were some great stories, which I'm sure Leon has told. We became really close mates and that created a team spirit that was remarkable - no team will ever be as good in my opinion - and with the fun and spirit we had as well as the talent, those years at St Helens were nothing short of magical.

People used to say we were the Harlem Globetrotters of rugby league at our peak, and I think Leon was a huge part of why we got that tag. It was the fun and the culture which made us so good, in my opinion. Fun was a huge part of our success at St

Helens. We loved being at training and Leon was the kind of guy who was great to have with you because there was lots of joking in and amongst the very serious preparation we undertook.

It was normally always hilarious - apart from the one time I was sat on the massage table and Leon was playing darts in our social area. One minute I was enjoying a nice relaxing neck massage, the next I saw I had a dart stuck in my leg - and it wasn't just in, it was stuck deep in my thigh, dangling out of my leg, as you do!

I look across the room and Leon was stood there laughing. 'What the hell are you thinking,' I asked. He said he wanted to know how close he could get a dart to my leg from so far away - it was pretty fucking close as it turned out! He threw it like a rocket from about seven metres away and bang, straight into my leg!

Luckily the club doctor was in that day and I had to have a tetanus injection and a week's worth of antibiotics! Cheers Leon! I could go on all day about the crazy stories both on and off the pitch, but I'm sure Leon will go over them in his own way throughout this book.

He's a terrific human being and he's great with kids - he has this way of talking to kids like they're grown-ups and he listens - and in return, they listen back. He's just a great bloke. He makes all people feel good about themselves and he genuinely cares for those who love him.

And I certainly love him.

# CHAPTER XVIII

The more I spoke to Trent Robinson and the more I learned about Catalans Dragons, what they wanted to do with me and the opportunity to become the first Englishman to play for the club, we began to speak to them in much closer detail. I went to meet Trent and I got the impression straight away that he was really, really keen on me coming over - and I like to be wanted as a player and a person.

The numbers were done fairly quickly and after weighing up the opportunity to hand my children and my wife a chance to experience a different culture, Catalans quickly became the more interesting and, dare I say it, appealing option as opposed to going back to the Bulls.

They had a new, exciting young coach who was taking the club in an interesting direction and from going over there as a St Helens player, I did think it would be nice to be getting cheered by all those crazy French fans rather than them jeering me as an opposition player!

I've spoken about how Daniel Anderson is the number one influence on my career in terms of people who I have played with or been coached by, but Trent was definitely second - it's not bad being second to Daniel Anderson either, let me say. The respect I have for Trent is on par with Daniel because he was just a great human being.

I think he spoke to Daniel at great length about signing me for Catalans and Daniel must have given me a good review. We had such a good year in that first season and having spoken about how Daniel knew how to manage people, the same was true for

Trent. He just treated people in the right way and he was able to assemble a team which could compete at the top that wasn't necessarily packed with world-class, unbelievable players.

He got players who wanted to prove themselves - while still being good players, of course - and he was the first coach that taught me how to manage players. Usually, coaches go into a market and look for the marquee names when they're looking for players. They might look at who is available and see a superb name and decide to sign him. But Trent taught me that you can't do that because, sometimes, it doesn't work that way.

What you need to do is sign players who fit your system. If you want to be a team where your back-rowers get the ball to the centres and promote good, expansive rugby, what's the point in signing a back-rower who, despite being a big name, can only hit good lines and has no hands? It doesn't fit.

He needed a half-back who could run because he had a scrum-half in Scott Dureau who could dominate the game and orchestrate a match. So I fitted into what Trent wanted, as did Steve Menzies, because he was that aforementioned back-rower who could score tries and set things up for his outside backs.

He signed Ian Henderson because he wanted to play with a dummy-half who could run with the ball and make breaks rather than be methodical - all of this added up to why we did so well. He needed players who wanted to prove a point, so guys like Lopini Paea, Scott Dureau and Daryl Millard were all quickly part of a team that got us to finish fourth, the highest Catalans have ever finished in Super League.

French players like David Ferriol, Thomas Bosc, Remi Casty,

Jason Baitieri and Vincent Duport were all really good players, who were at the core of the team too.

It's no coincidence that Trent had that success with those players and if you look at the squads Catalans have had since he went back to Australia, it's been very much about big-name players there - but that's not always what it's about in rugby league. Me as a player - and a coach - I will use that recruitment policy that Trent introduced to Catalans. He coached me well, he had beautiful, brilliant tactics I've never seen before and he decided we'd just play rugby. If there were overlaps, then we'd take them; if there was an option on the short side, then we'd take it. He got skilful players into the core of his team to work on attack and it definitely worked.

I didn't necessarily feel getting away from Bradford was essential at that time in my life, but the more I thought about it, the more positives stacked up in favour of going to Catalans. The culture, the lifestyle, the chance for my family to do something new - it was a really good move that not many people get the chance to do. The Bradford opportunity was great, don't get me wrong, and who knows what would have happened if I'd taken it, but Catalans was the better option for my family and my life when it all came around at that time. I don't regret going to Catalans one bit.

Before I signed, it was essentially down to Bradford and Catalans, but what also helped seal the deal was the fact that the Dragons laid down a three-year deal. Ask any rugby player what's important and they'll say a long deal, because it gives them security and a future.

I signed the deal shortly after that and my first game back for

St Helens after being out for 16 weeks was against, guess who, Catalans at Widnes! I was really nervous about coming back to play because I wasn't sure if my groin was going to hold up after that long-term injury, but I came on after about 55 minutes and it was really tight, and as I came onto the field and jogged onto the halfway line - because they'd just scored - the whole crowd went insane and they stood up applauding me. I couldn't hear myself think, that's how loud it was! I've never experienced anything like that before and that epitomised how they responded to me as a player. I know what I mean to them and I would just like to say to any St Helens fan reading this that you will always mean so much to me for little things like that, supporting me and feeling like you always had my back. I've done a lot of things in my career, but that is one of those special moments that I will hold with me forever. It was one of the most amazing feelings of my life. That was one day that solidified a lifelong relationship with St Helens: the town, the fans, the people - everything.

Anyway, after the game I was shaking hands with all the French lads and one of their overseas players, Clint Greenshields, marched towards me. I thought I'd done something wrong, but Clint wanted the inside track on whether I was going to Perpignan to play with him next year.

'Are you coming over next year mate,' he'd say. Eventually I had to give in. 'Yeah I am, but keep your mouth shut about it!'

Thankfully he did, but I'm just pleased I got the chance to leave St Helens on good terms too. I'm a bit of a hard-head and I like to do things on my own terms, so I probably would have liked to have had a bit more of a contribution towards the end of the year before I left, but things just didn't pan out that way.

Maybe I was a bit immature towards the back end with my thought process, who knows. I was stubborn and looking back, perhaps I was a bit naive about it all - but I only had myself to blame. I do wish I had stayed there for a bit longer, but as it all panned out, I'm a true believer that things happen for a reason and the experiences I would get in the years after leaving St Helens were spot on. I may not have won trophies, but as a family it really solidified us - it happened at the perfect time. I didn't make the squad for the Grand Final of 2011 against Leeds, and Royce Simmons went instead with Lee Gaskell and Jonny Lomax as his half-back pairing.

I knew nothing of Catalans and nothing of the place and Trent, other than when we played them. I wanted to know from the club whether they had schools where the children spoke English, because my two were nine and six at the time we were negotiating, so they needed to be happy more than anything.

It turned out there were no schools of that kind for miles, so after deliberating over it for a good while we ended up agreeing we'd put William - who was nine - into a school where everyone spoke French. That was actually my number one concern over moving, as I never actually went to Perpignan or to France until the day we moved. I didn't do any negotiating over there, it was all done in the Marriott in Leeds whenever Catalans had a game in England, which was every other week.

It wasn't easy to convince my family to make the move though. For example, Carly just didn't want to go as soon as I told her, she was dead against it. But the more we spoke about it and we weighed up our options, things just gradually fell into place for her, I think. The hot climate probably helped! But when you're in a bit of a fishbowl like Bradford it can become too much sometimes, and the opportunity to get away, just the four of us, to move to a different country, was a really good option for us to take up at that time. We loved each other, but our relationship wasn't solid, mine and Carly's, it wasn't tight. We felt like two individuals sometimes and it felt like a good time to start leading a good family life.

The kids were great with it, although they couldn't say much because they didn't have a choice in it! William struggled the hardest because they put him into a school where they didn't speak English, so for the first six months of our time over there he was practically shoved to the back of a classroom and just told to sit and write. That was obviously a bit of a concern for me, but gradually, it got better. The teacher he was left with wouldn't help him. She was awful, but as soon as he learned to speak French well enough, the rest of it became easy for him I think. I think he left having really enjoyed the experience.

There was Ian Henderson, who I'd played with at Bradford, who was over there and I knew, but that was about it. It was a strange old place on your own, just the four of us. But I liked the big deal they made out of my signing, to be honest, and I liked how they talked me up because I was the first ever Englishman to play for them. It gave me a really good motivation to do well there.

But my biggest problem as a person is my stubbornness really, and the thing about playing in France is that they like it when you try to integrate with the French, speak their language and live their way. Perhaps I didn't do that as well as I could have done over there, I guess.

We were awesome in the first season though. I thought I played some of the best rugby I'd played in my career and we finished fourth in the table. The club was a revelation under Trent's guidance, and I really enjoyed the rugby side of things straight away. The thing with rugby league is, whatever club you play for, that depends on the way you can be perceived in the press.

Being at the top clubs, the pressure is on a lot more and you often get a lot of praise, but when you're playing for a team like Catalans, sometimes you can't really see what they're doing all that often because they're plying their trade in a different country. It's a bit different now with all their games being on Sky Sports, but in that first year I thought I was playing just as well as when I was in my peak at St Helens - and maybe people couldn't see it compared to if I was still at Saints or a club like that, where you're on TV nearly every week.

I also wanted to play with Steve Menzies, if I'm being honest, as I knew he was there. I wanted to play with such a legend of the game and I'm really glad I did get the chance to do that. When I was mulling over whether to make the move to France, a really big part of what lured me to the Dragons was the chance to play with Steve.

He was there at the time and he's a massive name in rugby league and obviously if I'd stayed at Bradford my whole career, I would have got an opportunity to play alongside him a few years before he joined Catalans.

I ended up becoming good mates with Beaver. His wife and my wife bonded almost instantly too, which was great for her, to have friends in France while I was working. I don't think Carly was too happy that Beaver ended up getting me into golf and practically obsessed with it though, as it took up a lot of my time! When you get the chance to play with legendary players it's good to rub shoulders with them, but my best experiences with Beaver were away from the field - even though he's super-tight and he's mega-rich!

They just don't care about who you are in France either. I've mentioned about Bradford being a bit of a fishbowl and being a bit intense from time to time, especially if you're a well-known rugby player who has been known to make the wrong headlines now and again. But in France it was totally different. Yeah, in Perpignan they knew who the rugby players were, but they just treated them like everyone else - and you weren't pre-judged. They don't jump on things that you've done wrong. People over here like to look at the negative things you've done, but in France if you've done something in the past, so what? It's in the past.

Even though I was going in as the first Englishman to play for the club, there were obviously plenty of Australian boys in there who made the cultural shift a lot easier for me as a player and a person. Hendo was someone I knew well from my time at Bradford and other guys like Scott Dureau and Steve Menzies helped us all - and Steve's wife was similar to Carly with her interests, so that was nice, because they quickly formed a friendship which helped her settle in, I think.

But the people in France were beautiful, people like David Ferriol. I've a great story about Fef. When I played against him for St Helens he was renowned by some as a real dirty player and the kind of person who wanted to get under the skin of the opposition. He came to Saints in a game and he completely took my head off to such an extent where I needed a few stitches above my eye, because he absolutely whacked me! Every time

I played against him I used to think he was a horrible player and a horrible man. He used to elbow me, knee people and do all sorts, so the first day of training at Catalans, I was a little bit fearful of him!

Anyway, I stood up and admitted that I was pretty scared of Fef, because he had tried to kill me in the past while playing against him, and I didn't think he liked me very much for whatever reason!

Fef can't speak brilliant English, but he came over to me after the meeting and said, 'Leon, I'm so sorry, I did not mean it!'

'Don't be daft mate, you don't need to apologise,' I said, and since then, we've had a brilliant relationship. It all started so sour with him trying to decapitate me, but now I would class him as one of my better friends. If you know David Ferriol off the field you would know he is one of the nicest men you could ever have the privilege of meeting - even if he is nasty as hell on it!

But that's how he played the game, which I understand. I've got so much respect for him. He's got an amazing vineyard in France. When I married Carly I was playing for the Dragons, and he supplied all the wine for my wedding for absolutely free as a wedding present. He's the most generous, kind human being you could wish to meet, but his fire and his aggression on the field was a focal part of the Catalans team and the success we had. I love the bloke and I would love for him to truly know how much I value him as a friend - and it all came from him attacking me on a rugby field!

Another big difference was that at St Helens and Bradford we celebrated a win more often than not. We trained really hard and then had a beer after the game at the weekend, but when I went to Catalans, Trent wasn't quite as keen on the boys drinking. He wanted the drinking culture out of the way and it was definitely something I found to be a bit of a shock at first. I was finding it hard in the first year to find myself socially. I was used to having a lot of people around me like my friends who I spend time with off the field. That was a bit difficult to deal with at first too.

We eventually settled in a place called Saint-Cyprien, but for the first three or four months we lived in some apartments in the middle of Perpignan, in Canet. It was really quiet and it was really tough to adjust to, but that was part of why I wanted to go, to broaden my horizons. I'm very much a home bird and I love England and love Bradford, but those three years were great for me and my family. Life was just so much slower, but in a good way.

I remember shortly after we first got there that we went for something to eat. We turned up at 5pm and they said nowhere was open and we had to kick our heels waiting around for a couple of hours until they all bothered to open up at 7pm! Nothing, and I mean nothing, opened up until that time of night - it was so chilled and it was crazy, but it's a great place. It's a beautiful city with beautiful people and I had a great time playing there.

Bernard Guasch, the chairman, was very different to the other owners I've had, too. At the start of every season, all the players would head up to his hunting club - which he was always at - and we'd go shooting. We'd all be running around shooting pheasants for him.

He'd take you up to the top of the mountains in the morning - and I mean 5am, not just after the sun has come up! He'd ply you full of wine and have loads of bread, a proper breakfast, and you'd go around in groups of three with an experienced hunter alongside you.

You'd shoot about 120 pheasants which they let out during the course of the day. Then you'd go out, pick them up and you'd cook them with snails and have a proper French feast! He was such an awesome bloke. Stuff like that was so different to anything I'd done before. It turned out being a brilliant experience for me. I'd recommend it to anyone.

He was the boss of that club though - and he's why it's been so successful over the years. I've remained good friends with Bernard, but also with his son, Joan Guasch. I call him *petit chien*, which means 'little dog' in French, as he refers to me as 'big dog'! The whole family treated me very well, which was nice when we were trying to adjust to life over there.

As I've mentioned earlier in this book, it was at this stage of my career and my life where I could begin to move on from some of the horrible things that happened earlier, like the court cases and the off-field dickhead I used to be sometimes. It was that time in my life where I guess I had matured a bit, but I owe the French move a lot in relation to that.

The culture and the lifestyle of being in France - so different from home - was refreshing for me. I'm not trying to make out I'm the most famous bloke in the world, but when you're recognised everywhere around where you live, that can be a bit tiring on you. I'm a big, black guy and I stick out straight away. I can try and come across as really confident, but I am insecure.

People can give you mucky looks and I can dwell on the reactions of people, so to be somewhere where I just wasn't judged helped change me for the better.

I thought I could have easily done another two or three years at St Helens. And that year I signed for Catalans, was almost certainly going back to Bradford before that, the Bulls actually went into administration. So, looking back, it's the biggest relief of my life that I avoided that particular fate.

People always ask me what the travelling is like coming over to England every other week - and I've got to be honest, it was harder than we thought, certainly in the first season. Back then it was particularly tough because we had to get on the team bus at 6:30 in the morning and travel down to Girona to hop on a plane to England, and fly to Manchester or Leeds, before getting on a bus to wherever we were playing.

But in the second year, the club started chartering flights in and out of Perpignan Airport, which was massively helpful. We wouldn't be able to settle after training until 4:30pm in the afternoon in that first season though, which was a long day when you were getting ready for a game.

There were some strange moments surrounding the travelling, though. One week, we'd played Warrington on a Thursday or a Friday night and we stayed over in England before flying back to France the morning after, because you couldn't really get any great flights so late at night, especially when you had to get to an airport from a place like Warrington.

Over my time in France I made some good friends, and Brent Webb was definitely one of them. Playing against him on the field we disliked each other a lot. He was a niggly player too and so was I! We'd had a few bumps in a couple of games between Great Britain and New Zealand too, but from my experience, I never judge people how they are on the field because they're normally completely different off it - and that was definitely the case with Webby. In our time there together we became really good friends and he's one of the most genuine blokes I've ever met.

I used to room with him sometimes when we played games in England, and one time we got back to the hotel it was around midnight and we had to be up at something stupid like 4am or 5am to get on our flight back to France - and surprise, surprise, neither of us could get to sleep.

By this time, Webby has got his headphones in and he's doing press-ups like a maniac in our room - I'm not sure why, but it was funny! Knowing Webby like I do, he's a little bit crazy - just like me! Anyway, there were these things called 'brown bombers' which Webby had and they were super-strong sleeping tablets. I needed some semblance of sleep to function the day after and with it being just a few hours until we had to get up, I thought I'd bite the bullet, so to speak.

I'm watching Webby do his press-ups and he's going ballistic and I thought I was tripping, seriously! Sod it. 'Webby, chuck us one of them brown bombers of yours.'

'No,' he replies. 'Please Webby,' I say, 'I really need some kip mate.'

He replies, 'Leon, I can't give you one mate. They're just too strong'. Now I'd never had one before, so I didn't really believe him. So I kept demanding that he gave me one - it was only a sleeping tablet, what's the worst that could happen? Eventually he buckled, but it turns out he was right, they were bloody strong.

I can't remember anything about the following morning. We woke up at 5am and some of the lads had to physically drag me downstairs in my tracksuit. I just couldn't wake up. It was like I was a dead zombie. I was asleep all the way through the check-in desk, I was asleep sat at the table in the airport and all I can remember is that they tried to get me to the gate to get on the plane, but I remember being so tired that I couldn't keep my legs up and my body started to buckle underneath me. Suddenly, I had Daryl Millard and Lopini Paea behind me holding me up as I was dropping to the floor! They somehow got me on the plane without raising any suspicion and I slept all the way back to France - obviously!

When we got back to France, they took me to Webby's house and I think I slept straight through for well over a day, maybe a day and a half. I vaguely remember Carly coming in to look at me at one point, but I was out like a zombie and she had a face like thunder! Safe to say I never had one of these tablets again. It's funny looking back, but people don't realise how bad the sleeping is as a professional. You have two choices: you either buckle and take a tablet to get you to sleep so you feel okay the next day; or you don't, stay awake all night, because the adrenaline is still coursing through you, and feel half-dead the day after.

It's always a difficult decision to get right and there's never a right answer, I guess, is there? Especially with night games and even more so with Catalans, because half of your games involved travelling to England and back. You've got to learn to accept not to sleep or do what you can to sleep. The sleeping tablets aren't anything you should mess with. As humans we just need sleep sometimes and it's not like rugby players are the only people that take them, is it?

I went over there on a big contract and there was a lot of hype on me and a lot of expectation. Because we didn't win as often as they'd have liked, and I was pretty crappy with the way I played in the second year, it just made them unhappy as fans I think. It's not like I never feel pressure because I put pressure on myself - I'm not someone who can go and chill out. But I was expected to do good stuff there which I get, and despite it going so well in the first year, the second wasn't the best.

Maybe part of the reason for that was what happened with the coaching staff at the end of my first year in France, as Trent left to go back to Australia and Laurent Frayssinous - who was one of the two assistants alongside Jerome Guisset - got the head coaching job. I'd just had my knee cleaned out after playing against Hull when I found out Trent was going back. My knee was just locking time and time again. It happened against Leeds, which forced me to go up to Montpellier to have an operation to have some cartilage removed, when Trent rung me saying he had good news and bad news.

'I've been offered a deal by Sydney and I can't turn it down,' he said. Straight away I thought that it was great news for him yeah, but terrible for us.

After that, my relationship with Laurent was alright - well, it was until I left the Dragons anyway. I feel like I want to have my say on this, as it's something that is important to me. Basically, we were playing against Salford and afterwards, all the senior players were asked to go into the office and say what they thought about how things were going - and they were going pretty poorly at the time.

Laurent pulled me into the office, asked me why he thought we were losing games and what he thought we could change and, me being me, I just told him straight. I told him that the defensive efforts were rubbish - which they were - and if we didn't change that we just could not win games.

You don't have to be a rugby league expert to know that solid defence wins you games of rugby, but the way I came across, it must have been interpreted in his ears that we couldn't win with him coaching. It was massively lost in translation in my opinion, and when I went into training the next day, thinking we'd had a good chat and a good clearing of the air, we were split into the first-team squad and the second-team - my name was with the B squad, so straight away I knew something wasn't right.

It got to Friday, the day before the game, and Laurent pulled me into the office and he told me to go home - and not back to Saint-Cyprien, back to England. He said I would never play for Catalans Dragons again. This was about three or four weeks before the play-offs got going, I think it was in August. I'd already signed for Hull by then and the club knew, but I don't think it had anything to do with that whatsoever.

Carly ended up coming home to England almost straight away and I followed her soon after - and it was gutting, absolutely gutting, how it all ended in Perpignan for me and my family. I normally wouldn't have come home until the middle of October at the end of a season, but there we were, not even at the end of August, and I'm packing my bags, saying goodbye to friends and walking away without finishing the job at Catalans, all over a meeting that I thought was completely innocent.

I actually had to live with Ian Henderson for a couple of weeks, because we'd moved out of our apartment and until I could sort out the formalities of coming back to England myself, I needed somewhere to stay. That was how quickly it happened and how mad it all was. I went to speak to Bernard and he said it was the coach's decision and he had to back his coach, which I was fine with. I left on good terms with Bernard and it's probably why I went back in 2016 and was part of the 10-year celebrations: I just wasn't happy with how it came to an end with Laurent. At that event though, I managed to have a good chat with Laurent and put everything to bed about me leaving the Dragons and we're completely fine now, I've got to stress that.

Playing-wise, the first and third years were great for me. In that third year I was right in the running for the Albert Goldthorpe Medal. Well, I was in the running for it, until I was unceremoniously dropped!

All I was saying during that meeting was that if we continued to defend how we were, it was impossible for us to win anything - meaning a trophy. He took that as 'we can't win a game no matter what' and I don't know if he took it personally, but that is exactly what happened. It could easily be lost in translation like I say, but I was just telling him what I thought because I thought it would help us moving forward and I was, shall we say, removed from the team. But it is what it is, I guess - he had his reasons, rightly or wrongly, and you can't really go back.

When you're in France and you get the chance to play in the big events like Magic Weekend over in England, Catalans were ordinarily put with London, more often than not in the opening game of the weekend. There's never any fans, no atmosphere, no mood and even your average away game in Super League, you barely have any Catalans fans there because it's too expensive and time-consuming for them to get to England every single weekend. That was something I did miss if I'm being honest - the buzz of the big games and the old-school hostilities you get with English rugby league. I'd been used to big games like Bradford-Leeds and St Helens-Wigan and knowing I had a good three years ahead of me at the top level, and I knew I could still deliver.

That knee injury I got at Leeds right at the end of my first season in France was probably the pivotal turning point of my body's health for the rest of my career. I didn't think it would be at the time, but since then, when I've had that knee injury, I've never had the same spring in my leg than earlier in my career. It's madness. I just thought it was another injury, but it killed me. In the second season there, it was always sore and while I could manage playing with it, I just could never move the same ever again. I lost my sharpness and with the cartilage coming out, it's just bone that can't take any shock and it gets worse and worse.

I'd have liked to have done a couple more years there. I could have easily done another 12 months, no problem, if the circumstances weren't the same - and who knows, I'd probably go as far as saying it might have been my preference initially, because we had all felt part and parcel of the French life.

A lot of rugby league lads play for the same team and end up staying at one place throughout their whole career, because they feel like they're not being loyal if they move on. I found it quite strange when I did, because I played for Bradford for seven years before going to play for St Helens, Catalans and Hull, before coming back to Bradford. I think that sometimes, people wonder where your loyalties lie.

But I got great experiences from moving on to different clubs. Being from Bradford, your hometown team is generally the one you support and I never stopped being a Bradford supporter, but I learned so much from doing other things.

I still hold St Helens very close to my heart and the experience I got from moving to Catalans, and having all my family immerse themselves in French culture and things like that, was great. My son can now speak fluent French, which is obviously something I would have never been able to introduce him to if I'd stayed at Bradford my whole career. There's lots of positives from moving to different clubs and even though it's nice to be a one-club man, I found that career trajectory of mine to be hugely beneficial to me and my life. Catalans was definitely a big part of that.

I could have gone back to Bradford, but they had just been relegated to the Championship and out of Super League. I knew and I felt I had two more years as a Super League player in my legs and my body, so it's why eventually, Hull felt like the right move rather than going back to Bradford.

# CHAPTER XIX

I played with Lee Radford at Bradford for around seven or eight years, and he's always been a brilliant bloke with me and everyone who he's come into contact with - he's a very likeable guy. The way it came about was quite funny. When I was up for the charge years and years ago, I got a call while I was driving through Bradford, in an area called Lidget Green.

I pulled over, answered the phone and asked who it was. 'It's Steve,' this mysterious voice said. Ok. 'Steve who?' I replied. 'Steve Radford, Lee's father,' he said. He said to me that if anything happened with this court case, he promised I'd be looked after and I'd be alright. It doesn't sound much of a gesture to make, but when you're a 19-year-old kid and thinking that you might be going to jail, having someone take the time out to try and put your mind straight is pretty huge.

I've never forgotten that, and I've had a lot of respect for Steve since then and I've felt indebted to him and his family for that show of gratitude. I used to go across to Hull when I was a kid with Tevita Vaikona and I've played a lot of rugby over there, so I always knew how big a place it was and how big a club Hull FC was in particular. With Steve standing by me like that, and having always been good friends with Radders himself, I always thought that if I ever got the chance to play for Hull it would be great.

Ironically, it was after playing a game against Hull FC where the wheels really got set in motion. I was playing for Catalans and I had a pretty lengthy chat with Radders after the game about what I could offer to them, what he could give me and the whole package, really. They stayed in a hotel near us that night and it got done pretty quickly, as I recall.

I had a couple of offers from other clubs around that time too, so Hull weren't the only ones interested, even though it was tied up fairly quickly. I spoke to Daryl Powell at Castleford for one, but to be honest, my connection with Radders was really close due to the time we spent together at the Bulls. I could have got more money going to other clubs, but Hull just felt right.

As well as that, I also thought that for once in my life it was worth going with my heart rather than with my head. If it didn't work out, it didn't work out - at least I'd done what I thought was right. As it turned out I had a cracking time there and I did it for the right reasons - and I knew I was coming home no matter what at that time too, which always helped.

But I think in the run-up to joining Hull - a couple of years prior to that - I experienced probably the most defining moment of my entire career which would ultimately plague my time at Hull FC and the end of my Super League career. I was playing for Catalans - and ironically, it was against Hull FC. My knee locked up but straight away, it locked back out almost immediately and everything was fine - or so I thought. I had a bit of rehab on it in France and two weeks later we played Leeds and it completely locked again.

This time, I took a bit of a blow to the face by an opposition player and me being me, I ran and chased after the player because we made a break down the field - me being a hothead though, I was more interested in going after the bloke who had copped me one! As I was chasing him and I landed on his back, I slipped and my knee clicked and this time, it locked into place

- it didn't unlock. It was in a place where it wouldn't release and this guy turned around - I think he was going to hit me - and I was laid in the foetal position, begging for him not to hit me! I was almost in tears and luckily he didn't turn around and whack me, which he might have been within his rights to do after I hunted him down.

I got sent for a scan in Perpignan and I went to see someone in France who said there was nothing wrong with it, and that it would all be fine within a couple of weeks. Bear in mind that I couldn't move my knee from a 90-degree angle. Trent Robinson was fuming, going ballistic, because the diagnosis just wasn't right. So he got me sent up to Montpellier, a two-hour drive from Perpignan, to see a specialist.

They did one scan on it, looked at it for about 10 seconds, and said that I'd torn my meniscus and I needed an operation. By this point I had torn my adductor, had perforated a disc in my neck and had a reconstruction in my shoulder, and always played and been fine. I just assumed I'd have a knee cleanup and a few weeks afterwards, I'd be absolutely fine. But ever since I've had that, my running game has suffered really badly. I get pain in my knee all the time now. I always thought I would be fine, but the ground in Perpignan was generally really firm and given how I'm not the best trainer as it is, and not someone who does rehab really extensively, it affected me badly.

By the time I came to Hull, in God's honest truth it had gotten to a point where it was really sore on a near-daily basis. I could get through to games, but if I'm being honest with myself, my mind was probably starting to cash cheques that my body really couldn't. It affected my rugby and it disappointed me because in my mind, I still thought I could do it - but my body couldn't keep up with what my mind was thinking about.

First and foremost, as a player, I'm a runner. I like to come into the line and make breaks and it impacted on my game massively, compared to perhaps a half-back who passed and didn't take on the line as much. I'm making no excuses; I got offered deals by Castleford and Hull and I took £10,000 less to come and play for Hull because I wanted to play for Radders and I wanted to experience the Hull derby and things like that. He was a good mate of mine, Radders, but I ended up playing on the right side all the time - and I'm not a player who plays on any one side - I'm a floating half-back. I play a free role and that's one of the reasons why it didn't work out, but the biggest reason was due to my knee. I didn't hit the highest of what I expected of myself, but as a club and as people I formed some incredible relationships with them. I really miss seeing them on a daily basis, if I'm being honest.

Radders probably wanted to hammer it home that despite us being mates, he wanted to make it clear he was the boss, so he came down on me hard sometimes and he took things out on me that he wouldn't have done with anyone else. But I have a loud voice and a loud personality and he probably wanted to let me know he was the boss - which I don't blame him for one little bit. I'm not going to let it spoil my relationship with him because we're still great mates and I've got a world of respect for him as a coach.

When I came back to England from playing in France to sign for Hull, I settled back in quite quickly. It was great being back in England and back home, because we all moved straight back to Bradford in a house we'd kept during my time with Catalans.

My neighbours were great and they made us feel at home straight away - as this night I remember really well proves. One night, for whatever reason, I just couldn't sleep. I looked out of my window at around 4am in the morning and I was sure I could see a silhouette which looked like someone in my car, leaning over the seats and rooting around. I rubbed my eyes to make sure it wasn't just me who was seeing this, but sure enough, there was definitely someone in there. Shit!

Straight away I thought, 'I'm having this guy'. So I bolted from the window, tried to find my pants, but it was pitch black and I couldn't see anything - and obviously I didn't want to alert the burglar in the middle of the night. It was dark so I just ran downstairs with just a t-shirt on and nothing else on and then flew down the stairs and outside to try and get hold of him.

I opened my car and sure enough, there was someone in there rooting through my glove compartment, trying to nick some stuff I had in there - basically, whatever he could find. I grabbed him and slammed him up against the side of my car and started screaming at him, but I couldn't see him because he had a hood up and his face was all covered. I pulled him out of the car while I was half-naked and he tried to escape, so I didn't know what I was going to do next. On instinct, I screamed for my next-door neighbour Russell - this was at 4am in the morning on a quiet little street, bear in mind! I knew I could keep hold of him and I wasn't going to let him go, but having been in trouble previously, I didn't want to do anything to get myself into bother.

So, at the top of my voice, I shout, 'Russell! Russell!' Nobody knows what's going on and eventually, Russell's face appears at the window as this kid is still trying to escape. It took about five minutes, but he stormed downstairs with his dressing gown on and his bits flying everywhere - he won't mind me saying that! - and he pins this lad up against the car and ties him up! I didn't want to hurt him because I was gripping him, but Russell locked his arm behind him and slammed him into my car again!

By this time, my other neighbour, Immy, has come over and he's charged at this kid, lifted him up and slammed him into my car once again! I'm thinking, 'Jesus lads, be careful with my car!' All the while, Immy is taking photos of his face and playing vigilante!

I've still got my dick out flying everywhere, and Russell's wife Kirsty came out and she couldn't make eye contact with me because I had no pants on! So it was one of those awkward situations where, with two blokes wrestling a burglar behind me, we're trying not to look at each other! I've never known anything like it. I screamed for Carly to go and get me some shorts, but before she did, the whole street had come out to see me half naked. How embarrassing - nobody knew where to look, quite literally!

People always told me when I signed for Hull that the pressure there was huge and that it would be really difficult to deal with, but I've been going to Hull since I was 17, so I knew what I was in for, even if I'd never pulled an FC shirt on up until that point. It always felt a little bit easier living outside the city than in the middle of it, and that was always a plus for me.

I only ever really wanted to come back and live in Bradford, so doing that while playing for Hull obviously meant starting up the travelling again. I had to get another Yorkshire Bus cracking! There were some really good lads I travelled with though: Curtis Naughton, Joe Westerman, Liam Watts and even Gareth Ellis in the first year. We had some really good times together and it was a bit crazy - although not as crazy as that infamous bus that travelled to St Helens, I must admit!

Playing with younger lads like Jamie Shaul and Josh Bowden does alter your role too, and I knew I was going there as a bit of a leader and older head straight away, which I looked forward to.

But that style just meant I struggled to adapt in the first year there, and it was a new team with six or seven new players too. Plus, they weren't just new players in any old position. It was a new stand-off in myself, a new scrum-half in Marc Sneyd and a relatively new full-back in Jamie Shaul: it was a whole new spine. I think we struggled to play together. Me and Westy struggled and we were really finding it hard with our combinations and it was just a bit of a slog. It was a challenge from a playing perspective, but not everything can go right during your career of course and you learn from stuff like that even at the age I was then, well into my thirties.

Realistically, I went there knowing the challenge was to try and get them up the table and help establish them as the force I believed they could be within the sport, and although there's not too much I can say about the games I actually played in, the whole experience was sensational. When I had my knee operation at Catalans, my knee was so sore and it was slowing me down by the end of my first season at Hull and my game started to change as a result of it. I missed a few games more than I'd have liked to, but the fans and all the people at the club were just incredible with me, and I'll forever be thankful for that.

Most of my career had been an upward curve up until that point, but the Hull move was a real challenge - but as I said, you never stop learning. You've got to learn how to deal with adversity and how to deal with pressure and your game changing as a result of age and injuries. Missing big games, not being first on the team sheet is a big thing to deal with and I could have either kicked stones and been an arsehole or got on with it and find a way to accept that's life. I did the latter, I think, and I'm sure people at Hull would say the same. I'm pretty proud of how I handled myself in those two years there.

It was a difficult thing to adjust to initially, becoming more and more of a fringe player - although you quickly realise that every player experiences it, aside from maybe one or two. I played a few games in 2016 and I remember a moment where it hit me that I thought if I don't play that many games, I'm not that bothered.

Some people will be determined to keep their spot in the team even though they're slowing down, but as a half-back I remember stuff like trying to throw dummies and finding them harder to sell, and finding those gaps I used to slide through with ease now much tighter and much tougher. It's a sobering moment. You feel your body start to creak and ache a lot more and the game for me at that time became less enjoyable. I used to feel untouchable on a rugby field, but towards the back end at Hull, I sensed my time was beginning to come to an end. I was content with it though.

Once we knew that I wouldn't be staying in 2017, Lee pretty much decided he was going to play Carlos Tuimavave at stand-off for the rest of the 2016 season, which was completely his decision. They went to Australia and couldn't find a stand-off, so they opted for Carlos, and he ended up being the one.

At Magic Weekend that year, when we played Hull Kingston Rovers, a game I remember really well, they threw Carlos on from the bench and he helped set up four tries all on his own. After that, they obviously decided to give him four or five games to prove himself - which is fair enough - and after that it's difficult for me to come back in at the drop of a hat and show my worth, especially with everything I've mentioned about my knee slowing me down and things like that - but it's absolutely not an excuse. Like I say, I learned to deal with it and became stronger because of the adversity.

I hold my hand up. I didn't find my best form at Hull during those two years there. But I'll always hold the club in high regard and the lads there were absolutely brilliant, as were all the coaching staff I worked with. I felt as though I was a part of a good group of blokes and everyone got on really well.

Danny Houghton was someone I became really close with and I was delighted he got some accolades. Mint is a guy similar to me in that we would go into training and the first thing we would do is have a bit of a bitch and a whinge about something, and it could be anything! The weather might be crap, we might have to be doing loads of weights or someone could be annoying him, he'd love a moan and so would I and maybe that's why we got on so well! Two grumpy old men! But it was for banter, and the full squad was packed with blokes who knew how to have fun. Team spirit is something I've spoken about quite a lot throughout this book, and while we had it in spades at Hull, the one thing the club was missing was success.

That's why the first season was such a disappointment,

because it just never got going at any point for myself and the team - but year two, for the club at least, was great. I got into the team at the start of 2016, but if I'm being totally honest, I wasn't looking after myself properly off the field and away from rugby by this point. I should have done a better job of getting myself into better shape and that ultimately saw me get dropped and the rest is history. I had a great two years though and I will remember it for, like I say, the people who were there.

I also wanted to go there and change the perception of the way Hull were viewed in the wider world of rugby league, and Wembley definitely helped with that. I'm proud that I was there when guys like Danny Houghton - who has been consistently brilliant all throughout his career - finally got recognition and won the Man of Steel award. Gareth Ellis is another - his leadership was exceptional. Jamie Shaul and Marc Sneyd broke through and were on the verge of international honours in 2016, and really, that speaks volumes for the work everyone in that group did. Seeing that from an older, wiser perspective and someone who's been in the spotlight a lot, it's nice to see the hard work pay off for those guys.

The pinnacle of the two years, or the thing that was most notable, was undoubtedly Wembley. That itself as an experience for me just... well, it wasn't very nice, put it that way. It was a great experience for everyone in the group, of course it was, but it wasn't until two or three weeks after it where I could begin to let it go, given how I'd not played. In the immediate aftermath it was so tough though, honestly. I'd be sat at home on my phone looking at photos of the lads celebrating on the pitch and things like that, but one of them really smacked me in the face and woke me up from the sulk. There was a picture of Gaz Ellis, Mint (Houghton), Wattsy and Jamie Shaul and they were up on the walkway in the stadium. They were cheering and going berserk and I just remember looking at it and thinking that these lads had got to achieve something I've done a few times myself in the past - so stop being selfish Leon. Yeah, if you were playing you'd have got another one in the cabinet, but for those lads to win it for their club and for their city is something I got to do way back when with Bradford, and of course at a later date too with Saints, another club close to my heart.

But I didn't even go to the celebrations on the Monday after in the city - Radders knew I didn't feel right and he told me to have the day off if I wanted, and it was an easy decision to make. Personally I didn't want to be ruining anybody's day because I'd be walking around without a smile on my face and no real enjoyment in it, and I still stand by it now that it was the right thing to do. I loved that they got the chance to soak it in and drink it in because they got the monkey off the club's back and won at Wembley for the first time in their history.

It was just one of those things where I didn't feel properly part of the team, if that makes sense. I didn't feel like I deserved any credit, so I wanted to let the lads be the ones to enjoy their moment and I think Radders could sense it. For example, the night before the final, I went to bed really early. I've won five Challenge Cups before and even though I got a medal for playing during the run, the medal doesn't really mean a lot to me. In fact, it means nothing compared to the other ones because I played a role of significance in those triumphs. Did I really deserve a medal for sitting in the stands at Wembley and cheering them on? On that basis, you could have given 40,000

Hull fans medals. I wasn't on the field to do what they deserved, but selfishly, you obviously still want to be a part of it.

Afterwards, I didn't feel like I merited the opportunity to celebrate it. I played in the run-in to Wembley, but the way I work is that if I didn't contribute on the day, I won't hog the limelight. Everyone was trying to keep me involved as best as they possibly could and make me feel included, but it didn't matter how hard they tried - and they did - it just isn't my way to celebrate something I've not contributed to. Being on the field during the celebrations was the strangest part of it all to be honest - because that was their moment. In truth, I was in bed by 10:30pm on the night Hull FC won the Challenge Cup at Wembley.

I know people will only ever think about the 17 who played that day at Wembley, but I can at least look back with pride that I was involved in a group who achieved something very special - and with Radders, a Hull lad, as coach, and two more in Andy Last and Richard Horne alongside him in the backroom staff, the enormity of that season and that achievement should really never be forgotten. Even though I didn't play in that game at Wembley, I was part of the squad. For that, I'll forever be proud and forever be grateful.

That whole Wembley experience was probably the lowest moment in my rugby career though, I can't lie. It was a day where I didn't get a chance to play and I didn't even get to go on the team bus down to Wembley. I had to go on the one down there with all the wives and children of the players, so that was a pretty sobering moment. I didn't stay with the team and all that and by that point I had just had enough. It was easily the lowest ebb of my career. So I missed all the celebrations and came in refreshed. Radders gave me the captaincy for the game after Wembley and we played against Saints and that was nice. At the end of the day, they won the game against Warrington at Wembley, so it must have been the right call.

But when you're younger you get overawed really easily by massive occasions and massive stadiums. I remember going to places like Old Trafford, Twickenham and Wembley for the first time and thinking, 'Wow!' When you get older you stop taking everything in. When you walk into the ground you don't soak it up, you don't think about shaking hands, all you think about is getting into the sheds, doing your routine and preparing as you would any other game. You don't look at the crowd or anything like that, but I understand it's overwhelming for younger guys so you try and help those lads to deal with it a little bit.

I'd got used to not worrying about being in finals and dealing with the occasion, but this time, knowing I had no chance of being involved, I could look around and drink it all in a bit more, which was nice. For the first time in years I was relaxed, and I walked out of the tunnel and looked up and remember thinking, 'Jesus, this is massive!' I could appreciate it all in a totally different way.

Radders is a Hull kid. He's Hull through and through and he lives and breathes his rugby. Adam Pearson has to take plenty of credit for that too. There were lots of people within the media and even some fans who were calling for Radders' head in 2015, but Adam stuck to his guns and remained loyal to Lee and it shows you what a bit of loyalty can do in any walk of life. The good guys get their reward in the end. The club backed him and invested really well, but when you saw Radders lift that trophy up, it was a special moment and I was really proud and happy for him as a mate.

All in all, the main thing I took out of that two years there was that the group of lads reminded me of my time at Bradford. It was a group who loved playing rugby and loved spending time with each other. If you can surround yourself with people like that it makes training very easy and a great place to be - and that has a knock-on effect on the rest of the club, in my opinion. It was no surprise they did win something in that two years I was there. It was great to be a part of. If I'd retired at the end of 2016 having left Hull, I could have retired happy, I really could.

But by the time my first season there had ended in 2015, I knew even back then that I wouldn't be staying beyond 2016 at Hull - it became apparent fairly quickly to me. As I said, I played totally different to the way that suits Hull's system, even though I felt like I still had an influence on the place and the atmosphere in the camp.

But I was getting mentally tired and emotionally drained with playing Super League and there's only so many games you can play. I had 400-plus games under my belt and I realised I couldn't cash the cheques my mind was producing anymore. I remember playing one game at Warrington where, if I was three years younger, I would have had a hat-trick before half-time.

I just couldn't get that last little bit of acceleration through my legs to get me away like I used to - gaps I would have broken through and scored easily - and it's days like those where you realise your time is slowly coming to an end and your number is starting to come up. We were winning at the break in that game too and everyone was patting each other on the back and saying I had played well, but I knew in the back of my mind that a few years earlier, I would have probably had the man of the match award sewn up already.

They were laughing when I said I'd have scored a hat-trick in the first half, but I was deadly serious. I used to walk onto a field and feel like Superman and if I wanted to break through the line, a lot of the time I would be able to - simple as that. I started losing that air of invincibility and that was the time where I knew I either had to retire or accept I should drop down a level to the Championship in 2017. That's when it hit home, but as a club - the lads looked after me and treated me with respect - it was a brilliant experience and one that I definitely don't regret.

So then I started to think about what was next, obviously there was one place straight away that came into my thinking. Bradford has always been an option to me in one way or another every time I've moved clubs. I've been going back there and watching games since I left at the end of 2005, and when I left St Helens I was supposed to be going back there initially, but eventually I ended up opting to try something different in France with Catalans. Then when my time there came to an end I was all lined up to go back and play for the Bulls in 2015, but they got relegated that season so it was off the table. If they'd stayed up in 2014 I would have potentially gone there, but I knew I had another year or two left in me at the top level, so that quickly disappeared as an option.

Make no mistake about it though: I've always wanted to go back. At the end of the day I never left on my terms. I left on the premise that I wasn't being given as much of a chance in a particular position as I'd have liked. When great teams and great players are talked about in Bradford I don't think I'm ever in that bracket because I was just a utility player there. For me, I didn't feel like I achieved everything I wanted to. At Saints, with the great team we had, I was a pivotal part of it in the halves, but at the Bulls first time around, I was here, there and everywhere.

I honestly don't feel like I can be mentioned in the same breath as guys like Lesley Vainikolo, Shontayne Hape, Robbie Paul and people like that. It doesn't matter what other people think, I just never thought I fulfilled what I wanted to do at Bradford, so I always wanted to go back and put that right. I never thought I'd finish at Hull - whether I was 35, 45, 55 or crawling along the floor in old-age, I would always finish at Bradford. It was an unfinished chapter in my life that needed sorting out.

So as my time at Hull was winding down and I knew I needed a new club in 2016, I'd spoken to Robbie, Steve Ferres and Marc Green at numerous points about going back, and while there were other offers again on the table from other clubs, it comes to a point where it's not really about who's in charge at Odsal or anything like that. I was going back to my club to help out and do whatever I could to get them back to where we all felt they could be, which was Super League. I was more than sure I could go back there and do a job. Robbie left midway through 2016, of course, and he was a close friend, but I'd already signed the contract by then, so that didn't impact on things.

For my own legacy, I reckoned at that point I had one or two more years left in me when I signed the deal at Bradford. If I could get them up it would be a dream come true, but it's about more than that. My lad can come and watch me play for

Bradford and remember me in a Bulls shirt, and family can see me run around Odsal in a Bradford shirt all over again. However, the dream move back home couldn't really have started much worse.

# Danny Houghton

## (Hull FC teammate)

I remember before he came to Hull that when we did video sessions, he was the one player that we'd identify almost every time as a major threat and one of the opposition's most dangerous players. When he was at Saints he was one of those players where he played off the cuff and he was so big and imposing it was a situation where if you didn't handle Leon Pryce, you didn't handle St Helens: simple as that.

He's a legend of the game and he's a legend of the sport in my eyes. As a person and a friend he's even better. He's someone you couldn't ask anything more from too. He'll always have your back no matter what and that's a great quality for any person to have. He'd turn up to training with a spring in his step and a smile on his face and he'd just give everyone a real lift. He brought morale up during the two years he was at Hull FC all the time - it was a nice thing to have in a player who wasn't playing every week. Some people can sulk in that situation, but he definitely didn't - he helped to bring the best out of us.

I think he's a bit of a coach's nightmare though! Anyone who knows him knows what he's like. He's always chirping away in people's ears and always trying to wind folks up all the time and I can imagine that our gaffer, Lee Radford, probably hated it! But it's always in good spirits when he's winding people up - although he knows what he's doing 99 per cent of the time!

He'd probably openly admit that the two years he had here weren't the best of his career in terms of playing, but the bond he created with all of us was incredible. The group of players we have at Hull, we all take the piss out of each other, and Leon loves that. He loves to jump on that and wind people up and how people responded to his banter at Hull will have been really pleasing for him. I guess it's easy for someone to come into a new club and not really fit, but we all clicked with him and I think that made the tough times, like when he was injured or not playing, a lot easier.

He fitted into the surroundings really well and really easily, rather than people thinking, 'Who the hell does this guy think he is?'

We took to him well and he quickly became one of us. We knew he could take the banter and be jovial with it and not get on his high horse, which just made the group a better collective. The boys still speak about him even after he left Hull FC - and in a good, positive way I've got to add! He was massive for the club to be fair, because although his playing side wasn't the best years he's ever had, the bounce he brought to training was something you can't buy. And I guess when you bring people in, you can't gauge until they step through the door how good they'll be for the culture and the spirit you've got. Prycey added to it, without a shadow of a doubt.

Going into games, he brought almost an air of invincibility to the group where we felt like we couldn't be beaten, because he just gave us such a buzz and such a lift. We always speak about that, even after he's gone.

People will always associate the Wembley win in 2016, the first time Hull FC have won the Challenge Cup at Wembley, with the 17 blokes and Radders who did it on the day - but it's a squad game is rugby league. And that day sums the character Leon has to perfection, in my opinion. When he found out he wasn't playing he could have easily taken his bat and ball home and gone off and sulked - but he didn't.

Some people might have not wanted us to go on and win that cup, but he was right behind us every step of the way, and I think he was probably prouder than what some of the players were when we lifted that cup in the air at Wembley. That just typifies the guy he is, in my opinion.

I would say in terms of the best players in the Super League era, he's got to be in the top five. When he was at the top of his game he was destructive and almost untouchable at times. When he left Hull, he was still sending me clips of him from when he was at his best to remind me just how good he was at his peak! He does that on a regular basis, tries against Hull and going the full length of the field! But he was that good, he really was.

I guess it can be difficult with so many Hull lads to come into the group brand new, but with the stature and presence Leon has, you could easily judge early on that he was going to be brilliant for us. He might have had a bit of a chip on his shoulder, given how he'd been so good elsewhere, but there was none of that. From minute one, I took to him straight away and still now I class him as a really good friend of mine.

He still comes to training and I think he still wants to be one of us deep down! He comes over to see us with the Hull FC training gear on wanting to join in, I think he misses the banter and the camaraderie.

I could sum Leon up in one story. We were in Catalans during his first year at the club and he has this song all the fans sung for him, 'Na na na na na na, Leon Leon Pryce, Leon Pryce, Leon Leon Pryce!' - and Hull fans sung it too.

We'd been beaten on this occasion and Radders and the chairman were sat with us while we were having some pizza and a couple of beers at the golf course after the game like normal. We'd been told not to go crazy with the beer. Radders said have a few quiet ones, but it got quite wild! Anyway, Prycey falls asleep in his chair before everyone else, so we thought we'd sing his song to wake him up - and he bounces up out of his chair when he hears it!

He downs his pint, sits down and eventually falls back to sleep. All the lads looked at each other thinking, 'Is this guy for real?' We couldn't believe he just went back to sleep! So we sing the song again, and he bounces up again and downs his pint. Bearing in mind the chairman is sat within earshot of us all, he drinks his beer, slings the glass up in the air, it smashes all over the ceiling and he just walks off, goes to bed and the blame falls on us lads for causing a scene! That was him all over. Leon's great to be around and he's great fun.

The best way I could describe him is that he's a legend on the field and he's most definitely a legend off it too. We'll be mates forever. I'll always say he's a close friend. Sometimes you have friends in rugby when you're at a club and then you just say hello to each other when one moves on and you cross paths at a later date - but not Leon. He's someone I'll always make the effort to meet up with because he's one of the best blokes I've had the privilege of meeting.

# CHAPTER XX

I'd always kept my powder fairly dry on why I thought it all went wrong at Bradford throughout my career, but now feels like the right time to say my take. Essentially, I think it's important to point out that, in my opinion at least, it wasn't just one thing that people always refer to why it all went belly-up.

The whole demise of the Bradford Bulls revolves around a couple of key areas. The first for me was that, from the outside looking in, we simply stopped giving the players like Ryan Atkins and Chris Bridge a chance to prosper, where others had been given their opportunity in the past and taken it with both hands. We let myself go, we let Stuart Reardon go, Karl went to union and there were so many - Brett Ferres was another, Stuart Fielden went to Wigan, Rob Parker went to Salford, Lee Radford went to Hull.

There were a number of names there who have since gone on and had good careers in one way or another. We were signing players who were coming in at the back end of their careers who maybe had one or two years left in them. We let good, promising kids go as a result of that because they didn't have an opportunity to get into the first team and some of them ended up becoming future internationals for England.

This for me was the biggest reason why the Bulls went downhill. We signed Iestyn Harris when we did - and I want to make it clear that Iestyn is a great friend of mine and I've still got a good relationship with him to this day. Sometimes his name gets thrown at the wall as the sole reason when it really shouldn't do. The situation was this: we signed him knowing the legal situation behind it and when you do that and know that he may cost you hundreds of thousands of pounds if all goes wrong, the club only has themselves to blame, doesn't it? It's not Iestyn's fault, it's whoever made that decision.

I don't know the intricacies of it, but it's common knowledge that it cost the club a small fortune when it went through the courts. But at the same time, we made the single-biggest error that Bradford Bulls have made in the Super League era: we simply allowed Jamie Peacock to walk out of the door and join our biggest rivals, Leeds. How? How was this allowed to happen?

We had a captain who could have led the Bulls for the next 10 years, given the right contract being put on the table for him. Look at what he did after leaving Bradford at the end of 2005. He dominated the sport and, in hindsight, he still had his best years to come. It's an incredible decision, a staggering one. My opinion as a player and a fan was that it was the biggest regret the Bulls should have, letting JP go.

I'm not too sure if he definitely wanted to go to Leeds - I know it was his hometown club - but if we had offered him the contract that he deserved and he perhaps wanted to stay at Bradford, he would have hopefully taken it and signed on again. At the end of the day, he had already won the Man of Steel, he had already captained the Bulls and lifted silverware above his head in that shirt, so to me, we needed to invest our fortune into him.

I'm not saying don't sign Iestyn and offer the money to Jamie Peacock instead - I certainly wouldn't say that, because I thought on the field, Iestyn was a good signing for Bradford -

but I find it hard to believe that the club let JP just go for nothing. If they'd put him on a big enough deal and put him in a position where he had to sign, because it was too good to refuse, I don't think this whole mess would have ever happened - or certainly not as badly as it did.

He went on and won five or six Grand Finals while playing for Leeds, he became what I would believe to be the best forward in the world on several occasions and he could have spearheaded a new era at the Bulls, even if the likes of Robbie, myself and Stuart Reardon had all gone like we did at the end of 2005. It was a huge mistake by the Bulls.

The starting pack for England in the Four Nations in 2016 would have included people like Brett Ferres, Elliott Whitehead, John Bateman, the Burgess brothers - who, admittedly, would have probably still gone to the NRL - but it's still frightening to think they were all at Bradford at one time or another. The downfall is well-documented, of course it is, but it's more than one man's mistake, isn't it? It's a decade's worth of cock-ups, mismanagement and, most tellingly of all for me, not getting Jamie Peacock tied down. Did the legal battle over Iestyn cost the club a fortune? Of course it did, but don't tar Iestyn with the brush as the sole reason.

But despite all this, I was still looking forward to coming back to the Bulls in 2017. Even before I'd properly left Hull at the end of 2016, I already had started to think about how I would get myself ready for the move back to Bradford.

This was a move that meant a lot to me - and as anyone who's read this book all the way through will know, it's a move that I've been eyeing up for some years, but for whatever reason at whatever time, I just didn't come back.

It's the club I love, and have always loved since I was seven years old, when Phil Weston took me along to watch my first ever game of rugby league, stood on the terraces in the freezing cold watching Bradford Northern. He used to run me along to away games: Central Park, Naughton Park and some old-school grounds that aren't there anymore, and that's where I really caught the bug. I'd gone from fan to ballboy through to making my debut for the Bulls at the age of 16 - and here we are almost 20 years later, me getting to do it all again. I was buzzing.

Having always lived in Bradford, I could sense there was a nice buzz about me coming back and a real feeling of determination that we could challenge after a frustrating season in 2016. On two different occasions I'd had chances to come back that just didn't work out, for whatever reason, but this time, it really did feel like the right time given how I knew I wanted to finish my career at Bradford.

I just felt as though when I'd left Bradford in 2005, I had nowhere near fulfilled the potential I think I had as a top rugby league player. I didn't move clubs because I necessarily wanted to - although I'm so glad I did because I loved being at St Helens - but it was more because I had to, to further my career. I felt like I'd never left on my terms, to be honest.

The negotiations didn't really involve the coach at that time, Rohan Smith. I'd spoken to the likes of Marc Green, the then-chairman, and guys like Steve Ferres and Robbie who were all keen to see me come back to Odsal, which was nice. I felt wanted by them, so it didn't just feel like I was doing it for the sake of it. I'd actually signed the deal before Rohan arrived as coach, but by the time I started at the club in November 2016, Steve and Robbie had long since left the Bulls - there was just Marc Green left. Maybe they saw me coming, but by the time I'd arrived at the club, the whole place was totally different.

I had no idea that anything was wrong before I started, all seemed fine with the world. But after the very first field session we did with me back as a Bradford Bulls player, we came off the field having trained at Bradford Academy school and I got in my car and there were a few missed calls from people, as well as a few messages.

That wasn't normal and instantly you think something is up, so I went onto Twitter and scrolled down and saw a tweet saying Bradford Bulls were going into administration. I jumped out of my car and Rohan and Chev Walker - who was the assistant coach - were walking back up the road to get in their cars and I showed them it, not really sure whether they knew or not. Obviously they didn't, and they were as stunned as I was. From there, we went off in a panic down to our Tong training base and everyone was shell-shocked, saying that they couldn't believe it. Some of these lads had never experienced it before, but me being a Bradford lad, all I could think was, 'Oh no, it's happened again'.

We demanded to see Marc Green because the way we found out - via Twitter - was pretty disgraceful if I'm being honest. Imagine being in another walk of life and finding out your job is in jeopardy on the strength of what you see on social media. It was laughable, really.

Marc eventually turned up and we sat down with him and he

went through everything that had gone on; that he'd had some issues off the field with tax and we were in a position where if he didn't put the club into administration, then we would be going bust pretty much straight away. He said he wasn't expecting to be hit with the size of the bill he was and it was either administration or liquidation.

I was angry as hell because I'd found out off Twitter, so I said to him that the players simply had to find out first before anyone else. We had an open and honest chat about it and that was that. We all went on our way, off home to our families absolutely in shock. How do we break it to them? Jesus!

Anyway, as is standard with a club or a business going into administration, the administrators turned up shortly after that announcement. They got the keys to the ground and they essentially ran the business until they could find a buyer. From thereon out we were dealing with a guy called Gary Pettit and his solicitor as our first port of call.

I wasn't too angry with it all initially, because Gary came into a meeting with the players very bullishly - he was quite full of himself - and he started telling everybody that he's gone through these processes lots of times before and that it will all be sorted within two weeks. He said he had someone lined up, someone who was a big-timer and with plenty of money who could rejuvenate the Bulls, not just keep them alive. We were told he had plenty of experience and in a fortnight, it'll all be done and dusted. 'Fantastic, what a result,' I remember thinking.

I asked him a question about pay shortly after. We were in the middle of November and I wanted to know whether we'd be paid

- it would be tight, I knew that, but hopefully we would get the money. What would happen if it went into December though in regards to pay? 'That will not happen,' he said. 'There is no chance things will get that far without this all being sorted.'

I knew I was still due to be paid by Hull in November, so me personally, I was in a decent shape with my salary for that month because Hull FC never have a problem with paying you on time or anything like that, so that was all good.

RFL contracts run from December 1st to November 30th the following year, so the lads who were really worrying were the guys who were already under contract at Bradford in 2016. I was a bit more relaxed because Gary Pettit was telling me December wouldn't be a problem and I was getting my November money from Hull, so it felt all good. The way he was talking, he was giving it off that there was nothing to worry about, so I wasn't that angry in a strange kind of way - it settled everyone and reassured us - or it certainly did with me.

The players who had come up from London, such as Jon Magrin and Iliess Macani, as well as other new signings like Ross Peltier, had agreed - whether it was a gentleman's agreement or not, I don't know - that they would get an advance of their first month in the November period because they were moving up to play for the club.

It was essentially an advance they had been promised, so they spent their money as per normal, and when we went into administration these four or five lads went through the whole of the month with no wage whatsoever, not sure what was going on.

We weren't sure whether the lads would be paid at the end of

November, so it got to the point where we simply had to call a meeting. Some of the lads were suffering with anxiety really bad - one or two actually had some depression after it all - and they were in bits. One of the young lads came to me in tears about it all, it was horrible. Training was the last thing on their minds, understandably, so because I was a senior player they pulled me to one side and said they wanted me to speak with Rohan and find out exactly what was going on.

Now this was about three or four weeks after Gary Pettit had promised us it would all be sorted within a fortnight, so things were tense. In fact, it was the last time we'd seen him. Rohan came down and got Gary on the loudspeaker and we had a big long conversation with all the lads in the room, asking him all sorts of questions.

'To be honest lads, if things aren't sorted by Friday, then we're going to be putting the club into liquidation,' he said. What? There was a collective gasp and we all said we'd had enough of training without knowing if we'd been paid, so we just walked out.

We stuck together, every single one of us, and went for some food and a few drinks and tried to show some togetherness. We didn't train for a couple of days to clear our heads, but went back in on Saturday morning and things just weren't right, you could sense it.

But there were bigger issues at play which concerned me. As a player you're always insured by your club for any kind of injury - a sprained ankle, a broken leg, anything really - but there was no insurance in place for the players while we were training. So we were risking it all really. You would go to Bupa normally for your treatment, but that bill hadn't been paid and it was just an accumulation of things that were going wrong - like a snowball.

That messes with the players' heads and eventually we all came together after they didn't get paid in November - but eventually, three or four days later, it turned out there was enough money for them to be paid. That gave everyone a bit of a lift, so training in December was alright, but nobody had a clue what would be going on with the new owners.

We were essentially relying on what the fans were relying on: Twitter. One day we'd heard it would be a guy called David Thorne, the next we heard it might be Andrew Chalmers and we're constantly getting told not to worry, because there's 'at least' ten people interested in taking over the club. We're constantly refreshing our social media - I swear, this is all we were doing - and in our players' group chat on WhatsApp we were sharing messages and stories all the time which caused loads of confusion between one another.

Anyway, we struggled on through until the Christmas break and around that time players started to leave. James Clare left, Kris Welham went, Adam O'Brien and Alex Mellor went too and it naturally started to get quite heated.

We went through December and just before we broke up, every day was a different story. One day a certain new owner had been declined, then another day another guy dropped out - it was bedlam. Then we hear it's looking good, before this offer eventually falls through - and this is all coming from the mouths of the administrators. In December, when we were due to be paid our salaries and the club had not been put into liquidation, the administrators were then duty-bound to pay our wages, there was no other option for them.

Christmas was so stressful with it lingering in the back of our minds. It got to near the end of December, but because it was a Bank Holiday over into January, they would have had until the last day in December to pay us our wages. This time though, another Bank Holiday fell over New Year so they had even longer to sort it. That meant we went through the whole of Christmas and New Year not having a clue what was going on and on January 2nd, I got a call off Rohan, while I was sat on my couch, telling me that it had happened: the club was gone and had been liquidated. To be fair, I really appreciated him getting in touch and I put it straight into our group chat and drove down to Odsal.

I really wanted to see how the staff were. I mean we were players, we could probably sort ourselves out a club if we absolutely had to. But these guys had absolutely nothing - zilch. They're just as important as we are and they were all devastated, in tears and essentially in shock.

We went down to Tong as a playing group to see if anyone would show their face, but absolutely nobody turned up. I'm not sure who we were expecting to come to be honest. Maybe the administrator, I don't know. But eventually the solicitor of the administrators turned up because Gary Pettit had actually gone off on holiday. Don't forget he was the guy who had told us back in mid-November it would all be sorted within a fortnight and making us all sorts of promises, but someone else had to turn up and had to tell us to go home, because it was all over. 'You're done. Go start looking for jobs,' was essentially what we were told.

I never wanted to go anywhere else. My plan was to stay at Bradford, but it was in the back of my mind that if someone came in who wanted to make me surplus to requirements at a new Bradford Bulls, they could do that. I was just a free agent, don't forget, so they didn't *have* to sign me up on a new deal. It was turmoil. I had to think about my family and make some assurances that I could earn some money.

Anyway, we were all kicking around a few days after the club was liquidated and we suddenly got a message from someone saying to get up to Odsal because there was going to be a meeting with someone who wanted to revive the club - a New Zealand businessman called David Thorne. He sat us in a room and, to be fair to him, I couldn't fault the fact that he wanted to speak to the players that were left in person.

He made all sorts of assurances. He said Rohan would keep his job - as would all the players - and that we'd all be kept on our existing contracts moving forward. He told us that if he got the club, everything would be as it was and we'd continue as normal. He wanted to redevelop Odsal and make it a real force once again, so we left that meeting at Odsal and all collectively said, 'We want him to get it, this sounds awesome.'

As players, what else could we want? We were going to all keep our jobs on the same money and we'd be in a good place, but we ended up in limbo again for two or three weeks after that. I was speaking to Rohan for answers, but he was speaking to me in return and we ended up having no idea where we were going, especially with everything happening on social media.

I can't exactly remember how I found out that Andrew Chalmers and Graham Lowe had got it, but I remember it was a Friday when players were tweeting to see if they had a job - we had no idea until after it had been leaked in the press.

I was in contact with Ralph Rimmer from the RFL and I spoke to him because I was a senior player, and he said that he would be back in touch with me by the close of play on Friday afternoon, which to us meant 5pm. But it got to 5pm and I'd heard nothing, so I was looking on social media and on the BBC. There was a story at 5:15pm saying that Andrew and Graham had been given control of the new club and the chance to run it.

After everything that had happened over the last few months - being ignored, being lied to and everything - I had decided I'd had enough. I went on Twitter and put a tweet out saying I was trying to find out what was happening and I thought it was out of order that we as players didn't know first - surely that's only right?

I tweeted that and within minutes I'd had a text from Ralph saying that he'd seen my tweet and he'd sent an email to Rohan and Stuart Duffy at 5:40pm and they were the first to know - but how could they have been?

The BBC article was up live before any single person at the club got the opportunity to know what was happening - it summed the whole experience up for me. They were saying who it was going to be before we knew, so I'm getting all the players bricking it, asking me all sorts of questions like were we going to be full-time, did we have jobs and things like that. It was the first time we knew that David Thorne definitely wasn't getting the club and having been so encouraged by what he had to say, a bit of panic set in because we weren't sure of Andrew and Graham - apart from Graham's pedigree as a coach, of course.

Most of the lads were on Google trying to find out stuff about them, but I wasn't too fussed about that. Yes, it was a worrying time, but I was near the end of my career, and whatever happened, so be it. I'd decided by that point that I would probably retire if it all went wrong at Bradford or the new owners decided not to keep me on. I had jobs lined up outside of rugby league. A good friend of mine called Andrew Midgley works in recruitment and he was lining up all sorts of jobs for me.

I wanted to play for Bradford again, of course, but I had no other choice than to look elsewhere. I had no idea what they wanted to do with me - I thought I could have been hauled in there and told to piss off. They were calling players in one at a time to discuss their intentions with them and I was the first one in there, so I wasn't really sure what that meant. To be perfectly honest, they were top-class with me. I negotiated my own deal with them, we told each other what we thought and it was all done within 15 minutes and they told me they wanted me to be captain.

I'm very grateful I just managed to get something sorted, let alone being captain. I got the vibe from them in the meeting, but I was buzzing when they told me. It hit home when we had a press conference and I had to go up on stage and address everyone as Bradford captain alongside the new management and the new owners. It was a big day for the club and that was when I thought, yeah, this is a big deal.

It was very special and I just hope I can do the people of Bradford proud.

# WITH THANKS

Over my career I've had some really good support and a lot of help along the way. My close family, my friends and my children are right at the top of that, but I'd like to say that I did it all my way.

I could have probably got a bit more out of the game and a bit extra if I'd been a bit more dedicated to my training perhaps, but I've done it the way I wanted to and I've enjoyed doing that. I've probably not been the easiest guy to coach, but I've enjoyed rugby and enjoyed the fun it has brought - it's brought a lot more ups than downs.

It's been tough, but I've met some very good people along the way which have made the last 20 years really fun. I've met some really good blokes.

To my mum, my dad, my coaches and my teammates, I just want to say thanks. I've achieved quite a few individual awards in the game, but I've been fortunate to play in good teams - especially earlier on in my career. I was lucky I came into a Bradford team that were so successful and as well as playing a lot of games, I've got a lot to be thankful for.

To people like Brian Noble, Daniel Anderson and Trent Robinson for helping my career the way they did, thank you.

The most important part of succeeding is having a strong support - and your family are definitely that. Without them, my life would have been so much harder. Mum, Dad, Carly, Karl, everyone: thank you for the help you've given me away from rugby. Playing rugby would have been a lot harder without your support.

The Whole Pryce family, Stuart Reardon, Gavin Buckley, Jan Kwaitkowski, Julian Haddock, Daniel Ramsden, Matt Brambani, Matthew Broadbent, Andy Wilcock, Carly's family: Lucy, Laura, Avril, and Andy.

# Fans of Leon

Ryan Andrews

David Archer

Liam Archer

Debbie Armitage

Peter John Barnes

John Arthur Barnes

Steven Bartlett

Ian Birchall

Peter Boulton

Steven Brannan

Mandy and Mick Broadbent

Bullbuilder

Debbie Bullock

Paul Butterworth

Chris Callaghan

Michael Carr

Sara Cooper

Carol Cooper

Keith Dack

William Danson

Gerard Dibb

Michael Drewery

Harry Eaves

George Fawthrop

Kate Fieldhouse

Stephen Forkes

Tom Foster

Andrea Fowler

Craig Garland

Adrian Gill

John Gledhill

Alexander Grundy

Mark Hanwell

Chris Harrison

Chris Harvey

Rachel Harvey

Mark Harvey

Chris Hatton

Lesley Carol Hayter

Darren Hindle

Graham Holmes

Bob Holmes (Papa)

Stuart Hull

Lee Hunt

Charlotte Jones

Nick Joy

Maz Karolia

John Kelly

Anthony Kendall

James Klenk

Chris Knott

Nathan Lamb

Hilary Langley

Rich Langley

Liam Leddy

The Lewis Family

Loretta-Clare Moorhouse

Steve Mower

Roger Parkinson

Clifton Pennington

David Poskett

Nick Pyrah

Alann Redmonds

Darren Redmonds

Chris Rich

Jordan James Richardson

Heather Rushworth

Kyle Scully

Scott Sexton

Daniel Sharp

Alan Sharp

Patricia Smith

Chris Smith

Rebekah Megan Smith

Lee Speight

Geoff Strettle

Glenn Thomis

Mick Tillotson

Tony Tudor

Richard Wadsworth

Mr David Waterhouse

Siân Weston

Graham Wiley

David Williams

Robert Wood

Stephen Wood

Adam Wright

Jim Young

Mike Young

FOR MORE TITLES FROM GREAT NORTHERN BOOKS

VISIT

WWW.GREATNORTHERNBOOKS.CO.UK